AIRBORNE
AT WAR

17th Division gliders on the way to
the Rhine./*IWM*

438th Troop Carrier Group
dropping the 507th Parachute
Infantry near Diersfordt./US Army

AIRBORNE
AT WAR

Napier Crookenden

LONDON

IAN ALLAN LTD

First published 1978

ISBN 0 7110   0771 3

Design by Anthony Wirkus

© Napier Crookenden 1978

Published by Ian Allan Ltd, Shepperton, Surrey;
and printed in the United Kingdom by
Ian Allan Printing Ltd

Contents

Left: British glider troops decide what to do next, after leaving their crashed Horsa./*IWM*

Acknowledgements

I have received a great deal of help in preparing this book. Two books published in Germany have been most useful and I am grateful to Oberst F. O. Winzel of the Bund Deutscher Fallschirmjäger for putting me in touch with their authors. Herr Heinz Austermann's excellent history of the German parachute engineers in World War II *Von Eben Emael bis Edewechter Damm* gave me much of value for the chapter on Eben Emael and Herr Ernst Martin Winterstein's moving account of *General Meindl und seine Fallschirmjäger* is a mine of information on the struggle for Crete. Both these authors were most

generous in sending me copies of their books and of many photographs. Mr Hans Teske was also most helpful.

Mr Marcel Comeau's book on his experiences in Greece and Crete *Operation Mercury* gives an exciting and vivid impression of what it was like to be an airman, caught up in the drama of Crete, and my account owes a lot to his helpful comments.

In the United States you can rely on a prompt and generous response to calls for help from the US Army's Audio-Visual Activity, whence Majors V. R. White and Bruce R. Eaton sent me many photographs. Equally helpful were the National Archives and Records Service and the public affairs officer of the XVIII Airborne Corps, Lieutenant Colonel Ron David. I was lucky too in having a real friend and agent in Washington, Lieutenant General Julian J. Ewell, who amongst other kindnesses persuaded Major General William M. Miley and Brigadier J. V. Phelps to send me their priceless copies of *Thunder from Heaven* and *The Talon crosses the Rhine*.

The dust cover of this book is taken from a fine picture in the Officers Mess of the Parachute Regiment and I am most grateful to the artist, David Shepherd and the Officers of the Regiment for permission to use it. No one in England can write military history without the ready, willing and efficient help of the Ministry of Defence Whitehall Library, where Mr J. C. Andrews and his staff in the old War Office Building and at the Royal United Services Institute for Defence Studies could not be more helpful. The same can be said of the Imperial War Museum, where Mr Robert Crawford and Mr James Lucas have guided me so effectively in my search for photographs, and Mr J. C. Darracott's advice on pictures has been invaluable.

Once again I have found a willing helper in Mr Fitch of the Parachute Regiment Museum and a good deal of the Rhine Crossing Chapter is based on the British Army of the Rhine Battlefield Tour folder *Operation Varsity*, kindly lent to me by the Staff College.

Andrew Snell drew the maps with great skill, from my smudged and almost indecipherable sketches and the book could never have reached the publisher without the patient, accurate and gently corrective work with a typewriter of Mrs Joyce Moore and my wife.

Introduction

On 31 March 1977 the only Airborne formation in the British Regular Army, the 16th Parachute Brigade, ceased to exist. This was effectively the end of British Airborne Forces, for although the three Regular battalions and three Territorial and Army Volunteer Reserve Battalions of the Parachute Regiment remain part of the British Army's order of battle, Great Britain now retains the capability of launching into battle from the air only one parachute battalion group, dependent on ground forces for its supporting arms and services. So ended the 37-years' life of British Airborne Forces. Raised in June 1940 and expanded by the end of World War 2 to three Airborne divisions, they have made a remarkable and distinctive contribution to the long history of the British Army. Like all fighting units with the privilege of selecting their men, they have sometimes excited jealousy among less fortunate soldiers, but there is no doubt of the high general average of their fighting qualities and of the special impetus given by Airborne training to physical hardness, skill at arms and a cheerful confidence of each man in his mates and all ranks in each other. Lord Nelson's captains were 'a band of brothers' and such a fraternal company certainly embraced every man in Airborne Forces.

Whether Great Britain is right or wrong so to reduce her Airborne arm is controversial. Given the disappearance of Empire, the narrowing of our NATO interests to the northern plain of Germany and North Norway, the sharp reductions in RAF transport aircraft and our usual peacetime indifference to national security, the end of British Airborne Forces was probably inevitable. Germany and France have certainly done much the same, but in the United States the 82nd and 101st Airborne Divisions each contain 18,000 parachute and helicopter-borne troops in a high state of readiness, while the Soviet Union maintains an Airborne force of no less than seven divisions.

This is no place for a discussion of modern defence thinking, but it is of interest to look back at some of the Airborne operations of World War 2, not to examine out-dated techniques, but to see what sort of spirit the Airborne assault developed in its soldiers and airmen and to compare the operations of the three nations who used them most often and effectively — Germany, Great Britain and the United States.

D-Day in Normandy and the Battle of Arnhem have been well covered in books and films, so I have taken five lesser-known operations, for this particular edition of *Airborne at War* — two German, one American and one combined British and American. The capture of the Fort at Eben Emael by German parachute engineers, landing by glider on top of the fort, startled the world in May 1940 and set the pattern for many subsequent glider assaults by both sides. Some of the same men took part a year later in the German *Sturmregiment's* attack on Maleme airfield at the western end of Crete — the key to the whole German assault and a gamble so nearly lost, as to make it one of the greatest of the many great dramas in the long, violent and bloodstained history of that island.

Then, as the war was ending and on the other side of the world, the United States' re-capture of Corregidor showed how the bold and unorthodox use of parachute troops solved a difficult problem and saved many lives. Finally the use of the XVIII Airborne Corps in the crossing of the Rhine by 21 Army Group produced the largest aerial armada ever seen, as two complete airborne divisions were landed in one lift and within 2½ hours. The already crumbling German resistance was shattered at a stroke. Some historians have questioned the use of this airborne sledge-hammer to crack such a battered nut, yet the casualties on the first day are comparable with Arnhem and D-Day and the crossings by the XII and XXX Corps might well have been slower and bloodier without the airborne operation.

EBEN EMAEL

The Germans Prepare

In the rough and lawless years after World War 1 many elements of the German police force in the east were armed and equipped as military units, able to back up the small 100,000-strong *Reichswehr*, in both external defence and internal order. One of these para-military police battalions, the General Göring Regiment of the Prussian *Landpolizei*, was transferred to the Luftwaffe on 1 October 1935 and in April 1938 found itself converted to the parachute role and moved to Stendal in Altmark under the command of Major Bräuer. This was the beginning of German Airborne Forces. An Army parachute battalion under Major Heidrich began to form at Stendal at the same time, but the Army's high command were never enthusiastic about this new and untried arm and put up little resistance to Hermann Göring's determination to keep this

Below: German parachute training in 1939 at Lippstadt./*Austermann*

new venture wholly within the Luftwaffe. However an army division, the 22nd, stationed in Lower Saxony and commanded by General-major Graf Sponeck, was ordered to begin training as an airlanding division.

In the same year, 1938, command and co-ordination of all Luftwaffe airborne troops was given to General Kurt Student and after a few days of rather sceptical thought on the future of this band of saboteurs, he began to grow enthusiastic about the real potential of assault from the sky. In Student the German airborne troops found the essential enthusiast and man of action, capable of wresting resources from the High Command and putting into effect his own ideas on tactics, techniques and equipment, just as two years later two other men, Browning and Lee, were to become the 'fathers' of British and American airborne forces. Brought up on a small estate in Prussia, Kurt Student had been a fighter-pilot through World War 1 and between the wars was the man responsible for the secret build-up of German military aviation in defiance of the Treaty of Versailles by the use of an airbase in Russia and the development of gliding as a national sport.

At Stendal he found the two parachute battalions in being and a parachute engineer battalion forming, one of whose platoons was commanded by Leutnant Witzig. A reasonably efficient parachute, the RZ16, was available and a first rate transport aircraft, the Junkers 52. *Die alte Frau Ju* had been used as a bomber in the Spanish Civil war by the German Condor Legion, but was now the work-horse of the Luftwaffe transport squadrons and the German civil airline, Lufthansa. Its three motors and its corrugated skin have made it almost as well known over the last forty years as the Douglas C-47 Dakota and the Ju52's reliability and rugged construction enabled it to land on rough fields and to operate with little technical backing. It had a crew of three, carried twelve parachutists and could fly at 130mph for 800 miles.

By 1938 preparations for war were well advanced and although few men knew the operational plans, a sense of urgency developed amongst all ranks and a feeling that time was running out. Under pressure from Student German airborne forces began to build up. In January 1939 the *Reichswehr* parachute battalion at Stendal was transferred to the Luftwaffe to

12 and handled well. Skilful pilots, and a large number were available from the glider schools all over the country, could put it down within 20 yards of an objective, helped by a braking plough, a tail parachute and in later models, braking rockets in the nose.

On the outbreak of war in September 1939 only one regiment of the 7th Air Division saw action in Poland in a ground role, but General Student was soon involved in planning for the campaign in the West. While Army Group A was to burst through the Ardennes towards the Somme, Army Group B had the task of protecting the right flank by penetrating the Belgium and Dutch frontier defences and occupying both Belgium and Holland. To General Student was given the tasks of seizing intact the vital crossings over the rivers Rhine, Waal and Maas, as well as the bridges over the Albert Canal, so that the tanks of Army Group B might speed on into Holland and Belgium.

In April 1940 one of his parachute battalions was dropped by companies in Norway, against his advice as he thought it might give away the shock effect of using parachute troops for the first time. By this time German Airborne Forces had risen in strength to 4,000 parachute troops in the five battalions of the 7th Air Division, 12,000 glider troops in the 22nd Infantry Division and 1,000 Ju52 transport aircraft.

Left: German 'dive' method of exit./*IWM*

form 2nd Battalion 1st Parachute Rifle Regiment. The parachute engineer battalion was almost complete and Nos 1 and 2 Transport Wings with 450 Ju52s were added to his command. This was now named the 7th Air Division and the parachute school at Stendal and an experimental unit at Darmstadt were put under Student's direction. The 22nd Airlanding Division with its 12,000 men in the three Regiments — 16th Oldenburg, 47th Luneburg and 65th Bremen — also came under Student's command and the design and production of a troop carrying glider, the DFS 230, was hurried on at Darmstadt.

In 1933 Dr Alexander Lippisch of the *Rhön-Rossiten Gesellschaft* at Munich had designed a glider to carry a meteorological laboratory and this had been successfully test-flown by Hanna Reitsch, a brilliant glider pilot. She was the holder of the 1931 world record for long distance gliding and continued to test-fly gliders of every sort and size to the end of World War 2. In 1938 this glider was seen by Generals Udet and Jeschonnek of the Luftwaffe, who were struck by its military potential, and the *Deutsche Forschungsanstalt für Segelflug*, part of the Rhön Rossiten Institute at Darmstadt, was given a contract to develop urgently a troop-carrying version.

By 1939 a prototype was flying and this glider was later built in large numbers by the Gotha Wagen factory. With an all-up weight of 3,000lb it had a payload of nearly 2,000lb and could carry ten men. Made of tubular steel framework with a fabric covering, it had a glide angle of 1 in

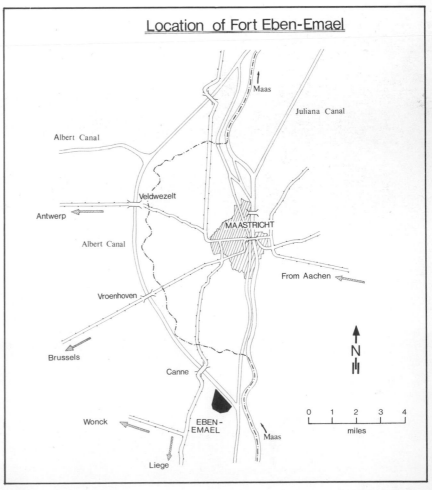

Location of Fort Eben-Emael

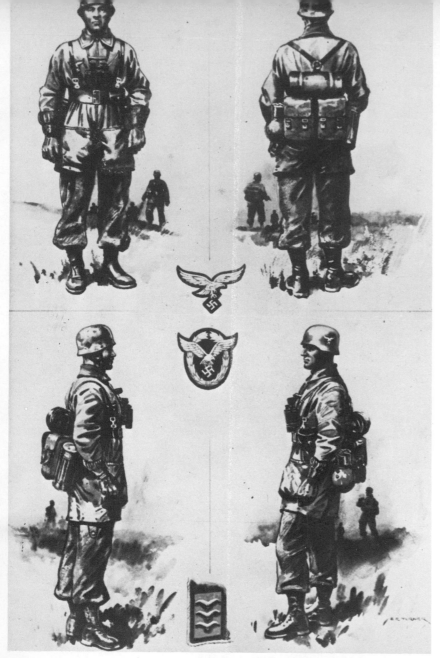

The five battalions of the 7th Air Division were to land by parachute on the bridges at Moerdijk and Rotterdam while the 22nd Division was to capture The Hague and seize the Dutch royal family, the government and the chiefs of staff. With the close support of the bomber and strike squadrons of the 2nd Air Fleet the bridges over the Maas and Waal were captured intact on 10 May 1940 and the German tanks pressed on into Holland. Inaccurate landings and fierce Dutch resistance brought failure and heavy casualties to the 22nd Division round The Hague and the Dutch royal family and government escaped in British destroyers.

For the seizure of the crossings over the Albert Canal into Belgium a special assault force, the *Sturmabteilung Koch* had been formed in November 1939 at Hildesheim. This consisted of No 1 Company of the 1st Parachute Rifle Regiment, an engineer platoon led by Leutnant Witzig, Oberleutnant Kiess's experimental DFS 230 gliders, 55 Ju52 aircraft, a searchlight platoon and an airfield service company, all under the command of Hauptmann Koch. The rifle company were given the job of capturing the three bridges over the canal at Vroenhoven, Veltwezelt and Canne, while Witzig's sapper platoon were to silence the fort at Eben Emael, which dominated these bridges and the road approaches from Maastricht.

Fort Eben Emael had been built between 1932 and 1935 at the junction of the River Maas and the Albert Canal, not far from where General von Kluck's 1st Army had crossed the Maas in 1914. It was designed to be impregnable and was sited on top of a hill with the sheer, 120ft, Albert Canal cutting to the north-east. On the north-west the fort dominated the low-lying over-flow area of the river Geer and both here and on the west and south twelve-foot walls faced a deep ditch. At each angle of the wall was a blockhouse from

Above: German parachute troops' equipment./*IWM*

Right: The anti-tank wall round the Fort./'*After the Battle*'

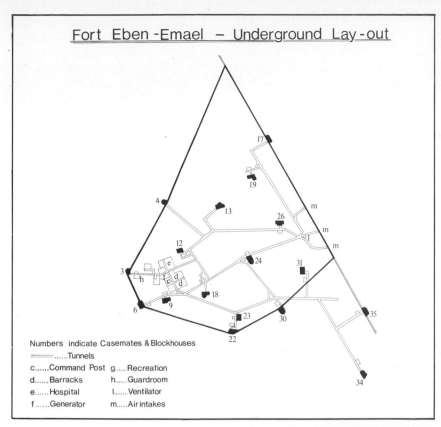

Fort Eben-Emael – Underground Lay-out

Numbers indicate Casemates & Blockhouses
══════ .....Tunnels
c......Command Post g......Recreation
d......Barracks h......Guardroom
e......Hospital l......Ventilator
f......Generator m.....Air intakes

Right: 50 kilo hollow-charge./*Austermann*

which machine guns and anti-tank guns could cover the river, the ditch and the approaches.

On top of the fort which was 1,200 yards from north to south and half a mile from east to west, were six batteries of 75mm guns and two machine gun positions, all fully protected under concrete and armour. The main punch of the fort was to be delivered by a pair of 120mm guns in a revolving turret. All these casements and positions had been spotted by German air reconnaissance, although two dummy casemates in the north were thought to be real.

Below the surface seven miles of tunnel linked the guns to the command post, hospital, workshop, signals centre, magazine and generator and on a lower level were the barracks and the air-conditioning plant. Every casemate could be sealed off from below and the fort was manned on 10 May by 650 officers and men under the command of Commandant Jottrand. There were another 233 men of the garrison off duty in the barracks at Wonck.

A stick of 12 parachute soldiers jumping from a Ju52 at an airspeed of 95mph from the minimum height of 300 feet would be spread over 300 yards. Their time of flight was about fifteen seconds and once on the ground it would be minutes before they could reach the machine guns and mortars in their containers. It was also difficult to make an accurate drop against pin-point targets. In contrast the DFS 230 glider, carrying ten men, could achieve a 20 kilometre range in silent flight, if released at 6,000 feet, and a good pilot could land it in daylight within 20 metres of a target. In these early days the Germans considered it essential to have daylight or plenty of flares for glider landings, although they were trained to drop by parachute in the dark. Hauptmann Koch decided therefore to attack the bridges with a mixed parachute and glider force, but to use gliders only to land his sapper platoon on top of Fort Eben Emael.

For the next six months the *Sturmabteilung Koch* planned and trained intensively for their task. They practised demolitions on Czech fortifications in the Adler mountains and on Polish emplacements near Gleiwitz. Detailed models of the bridges and the fort were made from air photos and deserters' accounts and intelligence reports about Eben Emael were carefully studied. Although two German firms had taken part in building the fort, the plans were not known in detail by the Germans and were certainly not available to Koch or Witzig. The glider pilots, men like Heiner Lange, Kartaus, Opitz, Brautigam, Raschke and Bredenbeck, all had long experience and had been carefully selected. They practised continually their pin-point landings and trained with all the weapons carried by the Group. Witzig's sappers exercised with flame-throwers, heavy explosive charges and ten-second fuses, but their best and most secret weapons were the specially designed hollow-charge explosives for the destruction of the Fort Eben Emael casemates. There were two of them, one of 50 kilos and another of 12½ kilos. The large charge was a half sphere with a steel lining and could be split into two for ease of carrying. On igniting, the force of explosion melted the steel liner and centred a jet of molten metal on to the casemate, driving a narrow hole through it up to a thickness of ten inches and shooting into the interior a lethal mixture of molten metal, hot gases and splinters. The smaller charge would penetrate six inches of armour plate and at greater thicknesses both charges could send flat scabs of metal whizzing off the inside surface.

Walter Koch divided his assault group into four, each with a codename. Leutnant Schacht and 96 men were to capture the bridge at Vroenhaven, codename 'Concrete'. 'Steel' meant the bridge at Veldwezelt, to be taken by Leutnant Altmann and 92 men. Leutnant Schächter with 92 men and the codename 'Iron' was to go for the bridge at Canne, while the engineer platoon led by

Fort Eben Emael: Surface Lay-out

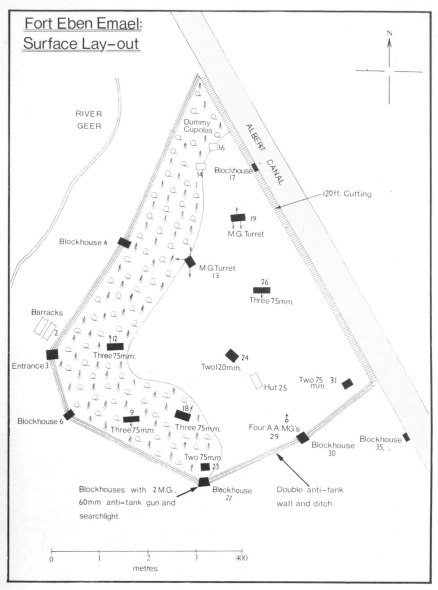

RIVER GEER

N

ALBERT CANAL

Dummy Cupolas

16

14

Blockhouse 17

120ft. Cutting

19

M.G. Turret

Blockhouse 4

M.G. Turret 13

26

Three 75mm.

Barracks

2

12

Three 75mm.

24

Two 120 m.m.

Hut 25

Two 75 m.m. 31

Entrance 3

Blockhouse 6

9

18

Three 75mm.

Three 75 m.m.

Four A.A. M.G's 29

Blockhouse 30

Blockhouse 35

Two 75mm.

23

Blockhouses with 2 M.G., 60mm anti-tank gun and searchlight.

Blockhouse 22

Double anti-tank wall and ditch.

0   1   2   3   400
metres

Leutnant Witzig had Fort Eben Emael as their objective with the codename 'Granite'.

Witzig was allotted 11 gliders and to each he detailed a section of seven or eight men under a *Feldwebel* with a specific task at the Fort. Each section carried a No 34 machine gun, a flamethrower, Schmeisser machine pistols, high explosive and smoke grenades, entrenching tools and a radio. Into the gliders were packed 28 50-kilo hollow-charges, 28 12½-kilo charges and a generous ration of pole charges and other explosives, to a total of two and a half tons.

To make sure that there was no breach of security, the gliders were dismantled and taken by road to the two take-off airfields near Cologne, Ostheim and Butzweilerhof. There they were concealed in locked and guarded hangars until the eve of D-Day, when they were assembled and checked. On 9 May the whole *Sturmabteilung Koch* received at long last the order to move from Hildesheim to their airfields and Rudolf Witzig has related the relief it was after six months of rigorous training and absolute seclusion. Take-off was to be at 4.30 on the morning of 10 May.

Oberjäger Erich Schuster has written vividly of their rush to prepare and load the gliders and to check parachutes, of the final briefings on their actual objectives and of how his own platoon commander Leutnant Gustav Altmann talked to them quietly and clearly about their task of capturing intact the bridge at Veltwezelt.

Rudolf Witzig had only 11 sections, each of eight men, to take on some 20 casemates and emplacements, manned by a garrison of 1,000 men. He gave them their jobs therefore, in an order of priority. Their first aim must be to destroy any weapons, which could fire on aircraft or gliders or sweep the top of the fort. This would include the anti-aircraft machine guns at Position 29, the concrete machine gun emplacements at 13 and 19 and the twin 75mm turrets at 23 and 31. Secondly they were to silence those gun batteries, which were sited to fire to the northwards on the three road bridges over the canal, the routes

forward of the German 4th Panzer Division. Finally he planned to blow in as many of the fort's entrances and exits as possible to prevent the garrison counter-attacking the 88 sappers on top of the fort.

Surprise and shock action were their main hopes and Witzig thought that they would probably have only an hour in which to act, before they were overwhelmed. The 51st Engineer Battalion, part of the 151st Infantry Regiment Group, the leading troops of 4th Panzer Division, were to cross the Albert Canal by the bridge at Canne on D-Day and to move at once to Fort Eben Emael to relieve and support Witzig's platoon and, if necessary, to attack and silence the fort. Flying in with the platoon was Leutnant Delica of the Luftwaffe, a forward air controller, able to call in by radio Ju87 dive-bombers, Me109 and 110 ground attack fighters and a pre-planned supply drop by Heinkel 111s.

By 8.40pm orders and briefings were complete and the men were told to fall out, write their wills and 'last letters' and make ready their equipment. Five minutes later a stream of 42 Ju52s began to land, filling the evening air with the noise of their motors, and taxi-ing from the runway to line up in echelon on the perimeter track. At the same time a field kitchen, pulled by two horses, drew up outside the hangar, where the men were checking their equipment, and everybody filled up with sausages, potatoes and coffee. At 9pm the hangar doors were opened and the ground crews pushed out the gliders, lined up each one behind its tug aircraft and connected up the tow-ropes. A little later the section commanders went round the men collecting their letters and wills and at 11.10 they marched out to the gliders. Each man was given a benzedrine tablet and then settled down by the gliders to sleep, to play cards and to while away the time until take-off.

Below: Air photo of the Fort, taken in 1974 by Mr Ramsey of *'After the Battle'./'After the Battle'*

The Glider Assault

At 2.30am on 10 May 1940 the leading tug aircraft and glider started down the runway and in 20 minutes all 42 of them were airborne from Ostheim and Butzweilerhof and setting course on their first leg to the south. Their route was marked at intervals by light beacons as far as the German frontier and once they had reached their planned altitude of 6,000 feet, they turned west and flew along the clearly visible line of beacons. Their route took them across the 'Dutch appendix' and as they flew over Maastricht, the Dutch anti-aircraft guns opened fire — probably the first shots of the 1940 campaign in the west.

By 4.05 the fort was in sight and at 4.10 the gliders were released from their tugs, the exact time planned to allow for an actual landing at 4.25am, five minutes before Army Groups A and B crossed the Dutch and Belgian frontiers.

Inside Fort Eben Emael an alert warning had been received from the Belgian headquarters at Liege at half past midnight by the sergeant of the guard, but although it spoke of German troop movements near the border, it caused no panic as it was the third 'alert' in a month. However the fort's commander, Commandant Jottrand, was woken up in his villa in the village and the fort garrison slowly came to life. Jottrand telephoned to Liege but could get no more information. Standing Orders for an 'Alert' called for 20 blank rounds from the 75mm guns of Cupola 31 at half-minute intervals, to warn the surrounding countryside and the canal bridge garrisons, but the crew only reached the guns at 3.30am. At 3.25 therefore, Captain Hotermans, who was in charge of all the guns, ordered Casemate 23 to fire the blanks, which they did. At about this time Jottrand heard gunfire from the direction of Maastricht and made up his mind that this was the real thing. He decided to clear and level the barrack huts outside the fort entrance, as was laid down in the 'Alert' plan, but as the off-duty shift were asleep in the billets at Wonck, he had to take men from the gun casements for this duty, leaving only skeleton crews in position and no one at all at the twin 75mm turret at Casemate 31.

By 3.15 the anti-aircraft machine guns in their open pits at Position 29 were manned and at 4 o'clock a report came in to Jottrand's command post from the bridge garrison at Canne: 'Fifty aircraft overhead at 5,000 feet'. Almost at once his own men from the top of the fort telephoned down to say that there were aircraft overhead with no engines and 'almost stopped in the air'. By now it was light enough to recognise the aircraft as gliders and Jottrand ordered all bridges and locks to be blown. Simultaneously the garrison at Vroenhaven reported: 'Aircraft landed near bridge. Shall we open fire?' At 4.15 the officers in the command post could hear no firing from their own guns and machine guns and Captain Hotermans rang Lieutenant Longdoz at Position 29 to ask the reason. Longdoz replied that they could not identify the aircraft, but on Hotermans's angry order, at once opened fire. Jottrand was also worried, because he had heard no explosions from the bridges. He rang Canne and was relieved to hear that the bridge was down, although the garrison was being attacked. There was no reply from Vroenhaven or Weltwezelt.

No 5 Section's glider was hit by Belgian machine gun fire, almost as soon as they had released from the tug. Heiner Lange, the pilot, put his glider into a dive to the south of the fort, flattened out near the ground and made a steep turn to the west below the level of the fort's south wall. Then he banked to the north, towards the anti-aircraft machine guns, their target, calling out a warning as he did so. The men packed in the fuselage behind him cocked their machine carbines and as Lange put the glider down, he caught one wing on the sandbags of a Belgian machine gun post, so that the whole glider swung round over the gun-pit. The four Belgians in the pit raised their hands, Lange jumped out of the glider and down into the pit, followed by a grenade from Feldwebel Haug — much to Lange's annoyance. The rest of the section piled out of the glider and in a few minutes had shot or captured all the Belgian gun crews. Haug then led his section off to attack his second objective, the twin 75mm gun turret at Position 23, but although he exploded a 50-kilo charge on top of the cupola, which rocked the gunners inside, the guns continued to fire for most of the day.

Feldwebel Neuhaus and his No 9 section had the job of silencing the steel and concrete machine gun emplacement at Position 13. Over Maastricht their glider had been badly shaken by Dutch anti-aircraft shells and was hit several times by machine gun fire from the fort. Schulz, their glider-pilot, landed them within 60 metres of Casement 13, but they found themselves in the middle of a barbed wire entanglement. Neuhaus

led his men through the wire using his wire-cutters and, on reaching the casemate, Schlosser put bursts of flame into the machine gun slits. They then put a 12½-kilo charge on the barrels and ran off. The Belgian crew inside could see what was happening through their observation cupola and were able to push the charge off the guns with a cleaning-rod, before it went off. Neuhaus and his men crawled back to the casemate again, threw grenades into the embrasures and fixed a 50-kilo hollow charge to the steel door. The explosion blew in both the door and the concrete door pillars, and so shocked the Belgians inside that they offered no resistance, as the Germans climbed in through the wreckage.

The second machine gun emplacement, covering the top of the fort, was at Position 19. From within the steel observation cupola Sergeants Vossen and Bataille saw the gliders land and ordered their gun crews to open fire. The job of silencing this casemate had been given to Oberfeldwebel Wenzel and No 4 Section and, after landing fairly near, they ran to the shelter of the casemate walls. Wenzel climbed up on top of it and set off a one-kilo charge on the periscope of the observation dome, but the machine guns below went on firing. Helped by another man he then placed a 50-kilo charge on top of the dome and although this explosion shook the gunners inside, it did not penetrate the armour plate. It was enough, however, to make the Belgians leave the casemate just as their commander, Sergeant Henrotay, came hurrying from the command post up the stairs from the tunnel. As he passed his scorched and shattered men, Wenzel outside detonated a second 50-kilo charge against one of the machine gun embrasures, blowing Henrotay back down the stairs and creating carnage and havoc in the casemate. Wenzel stepped through the smoking hole in the concrete to hear the telephone ringing. Lifting the receiver, he said in

English 'Here are Germans' and heard the reply 'Mon Dieu!' This casemate, 19, had been designated as platoon headquarters and Wenzel, the senior NCO of the platoon, now deployed his section in and around it. There was no sign of Leutnant Witzig.

The fourth and last of Witzig's priority targets was the twin 75mm gun turret at Position 31. This was the task for Feldwebel Unger's No 8 Section. Their glider-pilot, Diestelmeier, avoided the Belgian anti-aircraft machine guns by flying in a wide circle after release from his tug aircraft and coming in low and fast from the south. He brought his glider in to land most accurately only 30 metres from the gun turret at 31, but as the section got out, they came under heavy fire from Belgians in a long hut 100 metres away to the north. Ordering one of his men, Weinert, to cover him with the section's machine gun from a position near the glider, Unger, Hooge and Hierländer ran to the gun-turret to put a 50-kilo

17

Above: Casement 26. Three 75mm guns, facing south, knocked out by Feldwebel Hübel.

Right: The twin 120mm cupola at position 24.

charge on the steel dome and a 12½-kilo charge against the heavy steel door in the side of the casemate. Two more men, Else and Plitz, crawled toward the hut, whence the fire was coming, and exploded a 3-kilo charge at the door. Unger's two charges went off, badly shaking the gunners inside but doing no damage visible to the German sappers outside, so Unger set off another 50-kilo charge on the steel dome.

The Belgian crew had manned their guns by 3.30am and as the gliders landed they were seen from the observation cupola by Sergeants Kip and Joiris. They switched on the power, raised and traversed the turret, made a report of enemy near Casemate 19, but then had to lower the turret again, as the ammunition was still crated in the locked magazine and no one had the keys. When they were found, the ammunition hoist would not work, so Sergeant Hanot began to carry shells up the stairs in his arms. It was at this moment that Feldwebel Unger exploded a second 50-kilo charge on the dome, which wrenched the guns from their mountings, killed Sergeant Hanot, wounded several of the gun crews and damaged the turret control mechanism. One Belgian gunner continued to fire his machine gun from an embrasure, until silenced by a 2-kilo charge. At this moment shells began to fall round the casemate, probably from Casemate 23, Feldwebel Unger fell dead and his section, now led by Gefreiter Else moved off across the fort to join Wenzel at platoon headquarters near Casemate 19. At 5.45am Jottrand ordered that Casemate 31 be abandoned and the tunnel beneath it sealed off.

So in the first half hour the anti-aircraft machine guns at 29, both the machine gun casemates at 13 and 19 and one of the two twin 75mm turrets were out of action, and the surviving turret at 23 was firing with reduced accuracy and little observation. The German sappers had also crushed the Belgian machine gunners in the long hut near 25 and for a time were able to move freely about the top of the fort.

Two more sections had been detailed to silence the triple 75mm gun batteries, firing on the bridges to the north. One of these sections, led by Feldwebel Niedermeier, were in glider No 1 and from the moment they were released they could see the canal, the fort and their own objective, Casemate 18. Streams of tracer bullets converged on them and their glider-pilot, Raschke, took the same action as Lange and Diestelmeier, diving down almost to ground level south of the fort. Skimming over the ditch, pulling up over the south wall, he pancaked down to a rough landing close to the casemate. His wing broke off and in the rush to get out the Luftwaffe forward air controller, Delica, got jammed in the glider door. Then they were all out, but one of the men passing out the heavy explosive charges let one slip on to Niedermeier's head and stunned him for a few seconds.

Recovering quickly, Niedermeier ran on to the top of the casemate, carrying one half of a 50-kilo charge, followed by Druck with the other half. Quickly assembling the two halves, Niedermeier centred it exactly on top of the observation cupola, touched off the fuse and ran for cover. The explosion knocked him down, but killed both the Belgian sergeants inside the cupola, Marchoul and David. Two more German sappers, Kramer and Graef, now put a 12½-kilo charge against the casemate's steel door and the blast of the explosion smashed in the door, hurled the 75mm guns against the back wall of the casemate and killed three of the Belgian gunners, Philippe, Ferrire and Corporal Verbois. Niedermeier and two of his men jumped through the smashed door and fired a burst of Schmeisser fire down the stairwell. Outside the casemate the glider-pilot, Raschke, laid out the air recognition signals to make sure that they were not bombed by their own Stukas, and Druck went off to report success at platoon headquarters. Down below the Belgians set up a block in the tunnel leading to the shattered casemate and carried the burned and wounded men down to the hospital.

Feldwebel Arendt and his No 3 Section were to attack the 75mm guns in Casemate 12 to prevent them firing on the canal bridges to the north. His glider-pilot, Supper, had picked out the junction of the River Meuse and the Albert Canal, while they were still on tow. To make certain of his target he circled the fort twice after releasing from the tug and noticed no shooting, until he was almost on the casemate. Landing only 30 metres away, Arendt and his sappers were soon at the casemate, but could find no door and no observation dome. He also noticed to his surprise that the gun muzzles were coated with heavy preservation grease.

Having tried and failed to fix a 50-kilo charge to a gun port, Arendt and his section eventually lashed a 12½-kilo charge to the steel ball-joint at the root of the barrel. When it went off they were still too close, and were knocked flat by the blast. Black smoke poured out of a hole in the casemate front, a foot square, and groans could be heard inside. The gun had been torn from its mountings and thrown back into the casemate, crushing Gunner Borman, and on down to the bottom of the stair well. All the lights went out and a stack of propellant cartridges started to burn. Another gunner, Engelen, was thrown across the casemate into the telephone alcove and the rest of the crews

Above: Effect of a hollow-charge on the observation cupola at blockhouse 4./*'After the Battle'*

withdrew hastily down the stairs in a state of shock.

Arendt and two sappers, Kupsch and Stopp, slid through the hole feet first and found a number of wounded Belgians in the dark, smoke-filled interior. Down below Lieutenant Deuse was trying to organise a Belgian counter-attack and the sound of voices came up the stairs. Arendt dropped a 3-kilo explosive charge down the stair well, and after it had gone off with a terrific crash in the confined space of the tunnel below, no more was heard. A little later Arendt went cautiously down the stairway, counting up to 118 steps before he reached the bottom where he found a massive steel door.

Feldwebel Hübel's No 10 Section was in reserve and landed safely without casualties, although the glider had been hit several times by machine gun fire. His runner, Jürgerson, ran over to Casemate 19 to find platoon headquarters and Witzig, but only found Wenzel, who told him that there was no sign of the platoon commander or his glider crew and that Feldwebel Max Maier and his glider were also missing. Hübel was to attack the three 75mm guns, firing to the south from Casemate 26. In five minutes Hübel had blown in the observation cupola and all fire from these guns ceased for good at 4.50am.

The fort's most powerful guns, the 120mms in Casemate 24, had not yet been attacked. Their observer had seen the gliders land at 4.30 and the casemate commander, Sergeant Cremers, was ordered to engage the enemy in the area of the fort entrance. But when the gunners took post they found that they could not get at several vital parts for each gun and that there was no power on, so that the ammunition hoist and the electric rammers would not work. While the Belgian gun crews were struggling to remedy these faults, Heiner Lange, the glider-pilot from No 5 Section, came walking past Casemate 24 on his way to platoon headquarters with Belgian prisoners from

Delica, and he was neither trained nor eager to take over command — although after the battle he won the Knight's Cross of the Iron Cross for acting as platoon commander, Oberfeldwebel Wenzel, as the senior NCO, established platoon headquarters, set up the aid post for the wounded and made radio contact with Koch, the force commander at Vroenhaven. He also asked Delica to call in the dive-bombers on the fort entrance and to ask for the supply drop of ammunition by Heinkel 111 s. Two of these aircraft came over at about 600 feet soon after 7.30am and dropped their supplies on the southern part of the fort, which was still under fire. Wenzel ordered Heiner Lange, was was sitting nearby with his Belgian prisoners, to collect the supplies and bring them back behind Casemate 19. This they did without demur and without casualties.

The platoon had not done too badly. Both the machine gun casemates at 13 and 19; the two 75mm gun positions at 12 and 18 which could

the anti-aircraft positions. He watched the short, stubby barrels swing round towards him and thought he was about to be blown to pieces. Nothing happened except that a salvo of smaller shells landed close by, probably from Casemate 23, and Lange was hit in eight places by splinters. Ordering his prisoners to lie down, he ran to his glider near Position 29 and staggered back with both halves of a 50-kilo charge. Climbing on to the steel turret of the 120mm gun position he placed the charge, lit the fuse and ran — but the explosion caught him and deafened him for life. There was no effect on the turret. As Lange tried to pull himself together and to get his prisoners on the move, a soldier from his own section, Grechza, who had filled his water-bottle with rum the night before and was now happily drunk, climbed up on to the turret and rode astride one of the 120mm barrels, as the turret revolved. Wenzel now appeared on the scene and angrily ordered Grechza off the gun. He then set off a 3-kilo charge on each gun barrel, which shattered the Belgian gunners inside and put the casemate out of action. Two hours later the Belgian casemate commander, Sergeant Cremers, returned to the casemate and tried to fire the guns again. The first round split open one barrel and filled the casemate with smoke and fumes and when Lieutenant Dehousse arrived to check the guns, he reported them to Jottrand as unsafe to fire. They never fired again.

It was now half past six in the morning. Sixty-two German sappers had been on top of the fort for two hours. Two of them were dead, Feldwebel Unger hit by a shell splinter outside Casement 31 and Bögle in No 5 Section's attack on the anti-aircraft machine guns. Eight more were badly wounded and had been carried to platoon headquarters near Casemate 19. Four others had been hit more or less lightly and stayed with their sections. There was no sign of Leutnant Witzig or of Feldwebel Maier and their glider loads. The only German officer on the fort was Leutnant

20

fire to the north; and 26, one of the batteries firing to the south; the twin 75mm gun turret at 31; the anti-aircraft machine guns at 29; the Belgians in the hut at 25 and the two 120mm guns at 24 had all been put out of action. The twin turret at 23 was still firing, the blockhouses round the perimeter wall were generally intact and below, inside the fort, there were still over a thousand Belgians. There was no sign of the German 4th Panzer Division. Movement over the southern part of the fort's surface was risky and the German sappers began to feel the need for someone to take charge with a firm hand.

At about 8.30am a man at platoon headquarters shouted 'look up there' and they all saw a lone DFS 230 glider release from its tug and begin its descent towards the fort in a series of wide sweeps. Two minutes later it landed close by Casemate 19 and out stepped Leutnant Witzig.

Witzig's glider with Feldwebel Schwarz's reserve No 11 Section had been the last to take off. All went well as they climbed steadily towards their cruise altitude of 6,000 feet and the glider pilot, Gefreiter Pilz, checked off the pre-arranged turning points of a bonfire at Effern and a searchlight at Frechen. Suddenly their tug-aircraft went into a steep dive, apparently to avoid colliding with another aircraft. Pilz tried to follow, but the tow-rope broke and whipped back against the glider nose. They were miles from their objective and the prospect of missing the battle made them all curse and swear. Pilz turned back towards the Rhine and the Ostheim base, but a few minutes later he had to land in a grass field, not far from Cologne. This he did successfully without damaging the glider and Witzig at once set everyone to work, clearing fences and hedges to make a take-off run. He himself ran to the nearest village, where luckily there was an Army unit, roused them, borrowed a car and drove to Ostheim. It was now 4.05am. At the Operations Room they called up a Ju52 from

Götersich and an hour later Feldwebel Krutsch brought it into Ostheim. He picked up Witzig and a spare landing gear with a minimum of fuss and without stopping his engines, and in a few minutes they had taken off. Shortly afterwards they spotted the glider in a field, with its madly waving crew beside it. The Ju52 landed, with the help of some farm workers they lifted the glider and fitted the wheels, and minutes later the tug-glider combination was bouncing over the fields to a rough but successful take-off.

The other missing section, Feldwebel Maier's No 2, had been released too early and had landed near Düren. Commandeering a passing motor-cycle, Maier tried a police station and two Army barracks, until he finally succeeded in borrowing two staff cars from some army engineers. Piling in, they set off by road, threading their way through the long columns of tanks, trucks and marching men, through Maastricht and so to Canne, only to find the bridge blown and the German parachute troops of Storm Group Koch dug in on the far bank and engaged in a vigorous fire fight with the Belgian bridge garrison. Maier began to climb over the collapsed bridge, but was hit and mortally wounded by machine gun fire. His second in command, Gefreiter Meier, tried to cross along the sheltered side of the bridge, got over, stole a bicycle and pedalled furiously through the village of Eben Emael, passing columns of Belgian soldiers, who took no notice of him. A dive-bomb attack by Ju87 sent them all, including Meier, into the nearest ditch, but he finally reached the deserted Belgian barracks near the fort entrance. There he pulled a copy of daily orders off the notice board as proof he had been there, got shot at by men of Wenzel's section across the fort's ditch and eventually managed to contact Feldwebel Haug near No 4 Blockhouse.

Meier then went back to Canne to find his section, climbed back under shellfire across the broken bridge, and, as he did so, was wounded by a shell splinter. He never found his section but ended the day at the Bergen prisoner collecting point with 110 Belgian soldiers, whom he had rounded up in Canne.

Witzig was soon briefed by Wenzel and set off to visit his sections. At Casemate 12 he told Arendt to clear the woods to the north-west and silence No 4 blockhouse. This Arendt did by blowing a hole in the observation cupola with a 50-kilo charge, but on his return to Casemate 12 he came under fire from a Belgian patrol to the north-west and sent a runner, Merz, to ask Witzig for help. Witzig arrived promptly with six men and they all now faced south where a line of Belgians was emerging from the woods above the fort entrance. This was a first attempt at a counter-attack, led by Lieutenant De Sloovere, and a sharp engagement followed. The German sapper Merz was wounded in the arm by a grenade, Arendt tried to lead an attack on the Belgians but his section would not follow him, and almost at the same time, as so often happens,

21

the Belgians felt they had run out of both ammunition and steam and withdrew.

By 8am Jottrand in his command post below ground had realised how few Germans there were on top of him, but he was considerably shaken by the series of heavy explosions and the damage done to his casemates. Orders now came in by telephone from Liege for him to clear the top of the fort. Lieutenant De Sloovere's party were the first to try and Jottrand then told Lieutenant Verstraeten to collect volunteers for another attempt. With two sergeants and 12 soldiers, Verstraeten moved out of the fort entrance at Position 3 and along the ditch to the north towards Blockhouse 4. There he saw Arendt on top of the cupola, who disappeared before anyone could fire, and soon afterwards Verstraeten returned to the fort, much to Jottrand's fury. On being ordered at 9.30am to try again, Verstraeten and Sergeant l'Heureuse followed the same line as before, but on seeing some troops approaching from the west, they once again went back to the fort entrance. There they met those same troops, who turned out to be Captain Wagemans and 40 men of the Belgian 2nd Grenadiers. Wagemans asked for a guide and at 10.30 went off with his forty men and Lieutenant Deuse towards Blockhouse 4. Ju87 dive-bombers spotted them and attacked them several times, so that Wagemans spent most of the day near Blockhouse 4. On being refused shelter in the fort by Jottrand later in the day, he returned to his regiment that evening with little accomplished and a number of casualties. Meanwhile Verstraeten had moved out towards Casemate 12, but on being hit by a bullet, went back into the fort.

Earlier in the morning Jottrand had sent Lieutenant Mouton to check on the gun casemates and he had succeeded in climbing up into the shattered casemate 19. Mouton could hear Wenzel's men talking in German outside and returned to the command post. Jottrand now believed that most of his casemates were out of action and feared German penetration into the interior of the fort. He therefore ordered that all tunnels should be blocked by their steel barriers and sand-bag revetments and 18 of these barriers were set up. He also called for fire on to the surface of his own fort from the neighbouring forts of Pontisse and Barchon and these shells kept Witzig's men on the jump for most of the day.

Soon after midday Commandant Van der Auwera tried again to clear the surface of the fort and attacked Casemates 12 and 9 from the woods above the fort entrance. Only 25 men went with him and after a few bursts of fire from the Germans and a dive-bomb attack from the air, most of the men slipped back into the safety of the fort, leaving Van der Auwera with only three officers, one sergeant and four soldiers.

At 1pm Jottrand ordered his reserve at Wonck, three miles away, to counter-attack and clear the top of the fort. At 1.45pm Lieutenant Levaque marched out of Wonck with 233 men, but a series of Ju87 attacks scattered and delayed them so that by 4pm only Levaque and fifteen men had reached the fort. Some hours later, after dark, another 100 of his men turned up and joined the garrison in the fort. Levaque meanwhile collected 100 men from the fort garrison and made another attempt to clear Casemate 12, but as the light failed and the German machine gun fire caught them, only eight men stayed with him and by 6.45pm he was back inside. Here he met Captain Hotermans and in a mood of desperation they tried once more to reach the top, this time by moving along the tunnel to Blockhouse 4 where there was a second exit from the fort. Halfway along the tunnel they were bowled over by the blast of a big explosion ahead of them. Hotermans went forward to see what had happened and found a gaping hole in the roof of the blockhouse. Fearing a German attack through the blockhouse and into the tunnel, he left half his force to build a barrier there and returned to the command post with this further bit of bad news for Jottrand. It was now 7pm.

Throughout the day Witzig's chief concern was to prevent any Belgian counter-attack sweeping his small force off the top of the fort before the arrival of the German ground forces and in particular of the 51st Engineer Battalion, whose job it was to relieve him at Fort Eben Emael. Witzig had expected them to arrive during the morning and by midday he was beginning to wonder where they were. He knew by now that the bridges at Vroenhaven and Weltvezelt had been captured intact by the rest of the Koch Assault Group, but that the nearest bridge at Canne had been demolished by the Belgians. Early in the afternoon he told Feldwebel Harlos to silence Blockhouse 17 on the canal bank at the foot of the cutting on the east side of the fort, since this position could fire on attempts to cross the canal by boat. The Belgian gun crews in 17 did in fact have a busy and successful day, keeping up an intense fire from their machine guns and anti-tank gun against the leading elements of the German 151st Infantry Regiment and the 51st Engineer Battalion, as they closed up to the canal and tried to find places to cross it.

Blockhouse 17 was difficult to get at, built as it was into the bottom of the 120 foot cutting. Feldwebel Harlos tied three 50-kilo charges together and lowered them on a rope, until they were resting on top of the blockhouse. They went off with a colossal bang, but did no damage to the blockhouse or its crew. After two more tries, Harlos gave it up and the Belgians in Blockhouse 17 went on firing at the enemy until their position was blown in by the German 51st Engineers next morning.

While this was going on, Feldwebel Niedermeier asked Witzig if he could have a go at silencing the twin 75mm turret at 23, which was still firing at the German sappers on the fort and on the roads to the north. Niedermeier and his No 1 Section had destroyed the triple 75mm gun position at 18 and were inside the ruined casemate there, sheltering from the shells and machine gun fire still falling on the southern part of the fort. They were the closest German section to the turret at 23 and with three men, List, Graef and Stucke, Niedermeier crawled from 18 to 23 and watched the dome of the turret rising every two minutes to fire a salvo. Just as they were about to place a 50-kilo charge in position on the dome, three Ju87s made a dive-bomb attack on the turret and the four Germans ran for their lives back to Casemate 18 as the bombs burst all round them.

The leading regiment of the 4th Panzer Division, the 151st Infantry and its accompanying sapper battalion, the 51st, reached Canne in the late afternoon and some of them were across by 4pm. One platoon, led by Feldwebel Portsteffen, moved down the canal bank to a point opposite the fort, but their several attempts to cross by assault boat were driven back by the fire from Blockhouse 17. They finally got across after dark at about 10pm and moving round the north end, climbed up on to the top of the fort near Blockhouse 4.

In the early morning Witzig and Portsteffen made a joint plan, whereby Witzig's men would blow in as many stairways and tunnels below the gun casemates as they could, while Portsteffen and his platoon would attack the blockhouses in the perimeter wall. A series of heavy explosions followed and caused havoc down below. The lights failed, fumes and dust filled the tunnels and as the rest of the 51st Engineers came up, the blockhouses came under heavy anti-tank fire. Blockhouse 17 was blown up and at Casemate 12 Feldwebel Arendt touched off two 50-kilo charges in the stairwell, blowing the stair-shaft and ammunition hoist into a smoking ruin and sending a colossal blast wave along the tunnels below, blowing down a steel door and sending the Belgian defenders of the sandbag barricade behind it reeling back into the bowels of the fort.

By 10am on 11 May Witzig's tired sections in their various casemates had been relieved by the men of 51st Engineers and at noon Commandant Jottrand surrendered the fort. The men of Witzig's platoon paraded outside the fort entrance, where a long line of abandoned Belgian weapons and equipment lay on the ground. They had lost six men killed and 26 wounded, but they had a tremendous feeling of achievement. Witzig had radioed back to Hauptmann Koch asking for transport to meet them in the village and they marched down there at about 2pm. Witzig halted them at the village estaminet and they sat about on the chairs outside it, drinking beer and watching the Belgian garrison of the fort march by in a long column on their way into captivity. The trucks arrived, they climbed in and were back at Ostheim that evening. Soon afterwards the officers of *Sturmabteilung Koch* were summoned to meet Adolf Hitler, who decorated them with the Knight's Cross. Each soldier was given the Iron Cross by General Kesselring and they were all promoted one rank, except for the cheerful Grechza.

Koch was killed in a car accident on the autobahn in 1942. Witzig, Wenzel, Lange and many others fought in Crete, North Africa, Russia and Normandy. The news of the capture of Fort Eben Emael echoed round the world, and the exploits of these German parachute and glider troops in Holland and Belgium so impressed the British and Americans that they both began to raise their own Airborne troops in the following month of June 1940.

CRETE

The static line fully extended —
and another man about to jump.
Maleme, 20 May./*IWM*

Readiness

On 21 April 1941 General Papagos surrendered to the German Army and sixteen Greek divisions laid down their arms. Between 24 April and 1 May 50,672 British and Greek troops were evacuated from the mainland of Greece and most of them were taken to Crete, which the British Government had now decided to hold at all costs. On the same day as the Greek surrender Adolf Hitler held a conference at his Advanced Headquarters on the Semmering to discuss the next objective for the German forces in the eastern Mediterranean. Present at the conference were General Jodl, Generalfeldmarschall Keitel, General der Flieger Jeschonneck, and General der Flieger Student. They discussed the possibilities of launching an attack on Malta, on Crete or on Cyprus and finally agreed to General Student's dramatic and original proposal for an all-airborne invasion of Crete. Cyprus might follow and both islands would become springboards for the final assault on Egypt and the whole Allied position in the Middle East.

The XIth Air Corps began to move to Greece without delay by rail and road, while General Student stayed in Berlin with a small staff to complete his planning and to get the latest word from Admiral Canaris and the Intelligence Staff. Their view was that Crete was held by no more than one weak British division and some Greek battalions, all in a low state of morale after their crushing defeat in Greece. Student was also told that the Cretan population were looking forward to being liberated by the Germans and that a clandestine resistance group was waiting to help the German troops, as soon as they landed. In the next few weeks the German VIIIth Air Corps, who had played a major part in the Greek campaign, flew continuous reconnaissance over Crete and the seas round it, while the reconnaissance squadrons of the XIth Air Corps searched the island for dropping and landing zones and for British field defences, artillery positions and camps. The *Abwehr* stepped up its efforts to obtain information from agents in Crete and the many British prisoners of war in Greece were interrogated in detail. None of this changed the views of German intelligence and the resulting underestimate of British strength and fighting

Below: A troop train moving south through the Balkans in April 1941 — the horsed parachute soldier chasing 'Tommy'./IWM

Top right: A field kitchen on the same train.

Bottom right: German air photo of Maleme airfield.

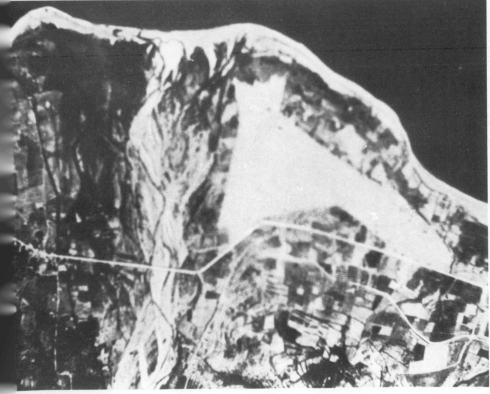

spirit came as a rude shock to the German airborne troops after their landings.

Air reconnaissance did disclose, however, that the only usable airfields with runways were at Maleme and Heraklion and that there was another smaller airfield at Rethymnon. There were strong anti-aircraft defences round these airfields and at Canea and Suda Bay, the capital and main port of the island. To the Oberkommando of the Luftwaffe and to General Student this was going to be very much an Air Force battle and it seemed that there were two choices open to them. They could land all their troops in the west of Crete and roll up the British garrison, as they advanced eastwards. This would have the advantage of a concentrated landing and the full support of the VIIIth Air Corps strike aircraft, but might result in a long and wearisome battle through the mountainous terrain of Crete with airfields in the east remaining much longer in British hands. This was the choice of Air Fleet 4, the senior Air Force formation in Greece. Alternatively they could make simultaneous landings at the four key points — the three airfields and the capital — so as to gain maximum surprise and shock effect and this was Student's choice. The final decision was to accept

Student's plan, and to ensure full protection and support from the VIIIth Air Corps bombers and fighters by launching a morning attack at Maleme and Canea and an afternoon landing at Rethymnon and Heraklion. General Student's XIth Air Corps included the 7th Air Division with its 1st, 2nd and 3rd Parachute Regiments and the Parachute Storm Regiment which had grown out of the Storm Detachment Koch, the captors of Fort Eben Emael in May 1940. Major Koch now commanded the 1st Battalion. The 7th Air Division's 1940 partners in the invasion of Holland, the Army's 22nd Air-landing Division, were deployed round the Ploesti oilfields in Roumania and so the 5th Mountain Division were put under General Student's command for the invasion of Crete, now called 'Operation Mercury'. This mountain division, led by Generalmajor Ringel, had fought throughout the campaign in Greece and had marched 1,500 kilometres in six weeks, mostly on their feet. They were not trained for air transport operations, but their light mountain equipment and their hard physical condition made them very suitable for the job in hand.

The outline plan was for the four battalions of the Parachute Storm Regiment under General Meindl to land in the early morning at Maleme to seize the airfield, while the 3rd Parachute Regiment under Oberst Heidrich would capture Canea. In the second wave on the afternoon of the same day the 1st and 2nd Parachute Regiments would drop on Heraklion and Rethymnon. The mountain division would follow up in transport aircraft to which ever airfield was secured first and two battalions of them were to go by sea in a mixed flotilla of motor boats, caiques and fishing boats. General Ringel has described how this whole plan, made at short notice and quite unlike any previous operation of war, 'sent cold shivers down my spine. The few sentences in my orders described with ominous brevity the most fiery ordeal, which man has ever had to face'.

These landings were to be covered and supported by the full strength of the VIIIth Air Corps and a programme of intensive preliminary attacks on the British in Crete was put into effect. Heinkel III and Dornier bombers, Ju87 dive-bombers and Me109 and 110 fighter bombers began to pound each and every target they could see.

Both the airborne troops and the mountain division were well trained and equipped and in high spirits after their victories in 1940 and 1941. The German Air Force had proved that they had the numbers, range, performance and armament to dominate the sky and to intervene decisively in the land battle. Yet there were a good many administrative headaches. The strike aircraft of the VIIIth Air Corps were deployed on nine airfields in southern Greece, Salonica, Bulgaria and Rhodes. The Ju52 transport aircraft were based at six airfields round Athens and Corinth.

There was no time to instal adequate telephone communications between these airfields and the headquarters of Air Fleet 4, VIIIth Air Corps and XIth Air Corps. Aviation fuel was in short supply, although the capture of 1,500 tons of British petrol at Athens had helped. Three ships bringing 9,000 tons of fuel from Italy were delayed by the activity of Allied submarines. There were very few bowsers and most of the aircraft had to be refuelled from 40-gallon drums, a slow and laborious process, and to make it worse there was only one, out of date, drum-filling plant in Athens. Another problem was the lack of metalled runways. Massed take-offs were almost impossible, because of the dust clouds stirred up by the propellors, and the use of fire-engines to moisten the dirt runways was never really effective. Improvisation was the order of the day, but in spite of commandeering most of the transport and much of the man-power from the Army divisions in Greece for the refuelling, it became essential to postpone D-Day first to 18 May and then to 20 May

On 16 May General Student gave out his orders to the regimental and battalion commanders of the 7th Air Division in the Hotel Grande Bretagne at Athens. Hauptmann Freiherr von der Heydte, commanding the 1st Battalion of

Below: General Ringel, commanding 5th Mountain Division talks to General Student, founder of German Airborne Forces and now commanding the XI Flieger Corps — taken near Canea later in the battle.

Bottom: Two Ju87 dive bombers over Crete.

Above: A photograph found on a German parachute soldier in Crete, taken on training in Germany, showing their jump boots, overalls and gloves./*IWM*

the 3rd Regiment, who was later to command the 6th Parachute Regiment against the American 101st Airborne Division in Normandy, has described the sealed and shuttered room, the large map of Crete on the wall and the General's clear, incisive and vibrant voice. He also remembers how the Corps Intelligence Officer confirmed the enemy garrison of Crete as being not more than one British division and a few Greek battalions.

General Meindl was given Maleme airfield as the objective for his Storm Regiment and his own orders to his battalions were short and simple. It was a firm principle in German Airborne Forces to tell each commander at each successive level his task and the troops allotted to him, and to leave to him the method and the tactics to be used. Major Koch's 1st Battalion were to detach 1 and 2 companies to the 3rd and 2nd Parachute Regiments for the destruction of anti-aircraft batteries at Suda and Rethymnon by glider attack, before the main parachute force came within range. His own headquarters with 3 and 4 companies were to land by glider at 8am on two landing zones in the Tavronitis river bed, immediately west of Maleme airfield and near the British tented camp south of the main road. They were to destroy the anti-aircraft guns on the airfield and on Hill 107 and to capture the tented camp. Five minutes later the 2nd Battalion under Major Stenzler would jump on the high ground to the west near Spilia to guard against enemy attacks from the west and to form a regimental reserve. A strong platoon of 80 men from the 2nd Battalion led by Leutnant Mürbe was to drop at the Kastelli cross-roads five miles to the west to

destroy a weak enemy unit, known to be stationed there.

At 8.15 the regimental headquarters, a parachute field ambulance, a section of parachute artillery and Hauptmann Gericke's 4th Battalion which was the heavy weapons and specialist unit of the regiment with a pioneer company, an anti-tank company, a heavy machine gun company and a mortar company, would drop by parachute just west of Tavronitis village and attack the airfield from the west. At the same time regimental headquarters defence platoon, led by Major Braun and including Oberleutnants Schachter and Trebes, were to land by glider as close as possible to the iron girder road bridge over the Tavronitis and to capture it intact. They were then to join up with the 1st Battalion. The 3rd Battalion, Major Scherber, were to drop at 8.30 on the flat ground north and south of Maleme and Pirgos villages. They were then to clear the villages and attack the airfield from the east.

By the evening of 19 May every unit of the 7th Air Division was encamped beside its take-off airfield. Erich Schuster, who had fought in Belgium and who was later killed in Tunisia, has left an account of that evening in 3 Company of the Storm Regiment's 1st Battalion. Oberleutnant von Plessen, their company commander, gave out his final orders to his platoon and section commanders with these words:

'Comrades, let's go through our tasks once more. We shall be three officers, 27 NCOs and 77 men tomorrow. The rest of the company under Oberleutnant Osius will form a force reserve.

There are 12 gliders for us, three for each platoon. Now, our job! I shall lead company headquarters against the small wood on the west edge of the airfield, where our air photos show enemy slit trenches. Leutnant Musyal, you and 1 Platoon will attack and destroy the anti-aircraft gun positions half a mile west of the runway. No 2 Platoon, Feldwebel Arpke, will take on the light anti-aircraft guns on the north and north-west edges of the airfield. Oberfeldwebel Scheel with No 3 Platoon, you will land at the south-west corner of the airfield and destroy any enemy there. Don't forget, our main task is to silence the anti-aircraft guns and machine guns as soon as we can, and so protect the main landing of our parachute battalions, who are following us in. When we have done this, the company will prevent any enemy attacks from the west by forming a defensive position on the west bank of the river from the seashore on our right to the main road on our left. We shall also patrol out to contact the 4th Battalion, who are dropping west of us, and we shall do what we can to clear the airfield of obstacles. That's it!'

Early next morning before sunrise the men left their bivouac tents on the perimeter of Eleusis airfield and paraded by sections. Their officers reported all correct to Von Plessen, who gave the order to emplane and, one behind the other, the sections marched to their gliders, already lined up behind their tug-aircraft with tow-ropes secured and checked. Oberfeldwebel Arpke poked his head into two of the three gliders of his platoon

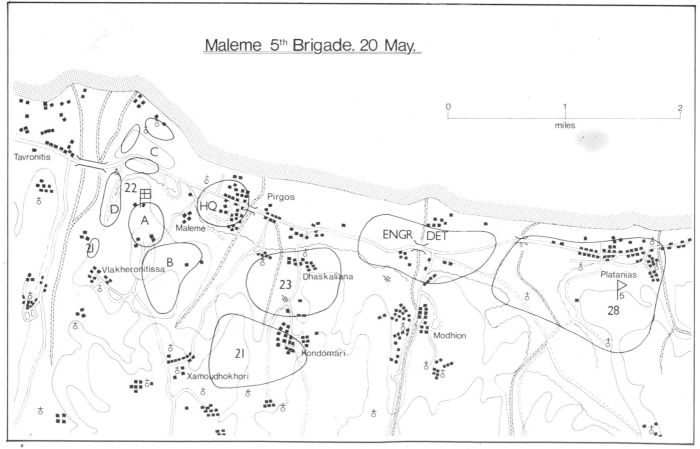

Maleme 5th Brigade. 20 May.

with a cheerful 'Do your stuff, men' before clambering into his own. Then at 6.30am all the Ju52s started their motors and the long column of aircraft and gliders began to move round towards the runway. On take-off each glider bumped along behind its tug and lifted off the ground. The landing wheels fell away, as they were jettisoned, and the runway disappeared behind them in a cloud of dust. Soon they were all airborne and moving into formation, as they climbed to their cruise altitude. As the sun came up over the horizon to their port side, they set course to the south for Crete.

By mid-May the British and Greek forces in Crete numbered about 42,100, made up of 15,000 men of the British Army, 400 sailors, mostly from the Fleet Air Arm, 2,000 marines of the Marine Naval Base Defence Organisation, 600 RAF ground staff on the three airfields, 6,500 Australians, the 2nd New Zealand Division of 7,700 men and some 10,300 Greeks. They were fit and rested after their exertions in Greece, but all units were short of wireless sets and heavy weapons and the Greek battalions did not have enough rifles and ammunition to go round. The General Officer Commanding, Major-General Freyberg, was a lion-hearted leader of men, who had won the VC in World War 1 and was to make the New Zealand Division into one of the best infantry divisions in the Allied armies. He knew well from the accurate intelligence coming out of Greece, that the Germans were building up a massive airborne assault force; he judged

accurately that their main landing zones must be at Maleme, Canea, Rethymnon and Heraklion and he deployed his forces accordingly. His intelligence staffs forecast that the Germans would attack on 15 or 16 May. On 18 May the surviving aircrew of a German Dornier, shot down near Suda Bay, boasted to their captors that they would be freed on the 20th. Within the limits of the available resources of men and guns, the island's garrison were ready for the Germans and were generally eager to see them off.

Responsibility for the defence of the western sector of the island was given by Freyberg to the New Zealand Division and their commander, Brigadier Puttick. In his turn Puttick told his 5th New Zealand Infantry Brigade, commanded by Brigadier Hargest, to hold Maleme airfield and the coast from the mouth of the Tavronitis river to Platanias, five miles to the east. They were all expecting both airborne and seaborne attack and thought that the German parachute and glider troops and even their Ju52 transport aircraft might force-land on any reasonably open space. Hargest therefore placed his battalions to cover the whole area, with his 22nd Battalion at Maleme, the 23rd and 21st two miles to the east on the higher ground overlooking the coastal plain, his engineers in the middle of the area and the 28th Maori Battalion with brigade headquarters at Platanias.

The 22nd New Zealand Infantry Battalion, 620 men strong, was commanded by Lieutenant Colonel Andrew. He was forty-four years old and

Top left: General Meindl, commanding the Sturmregiment, discussing the plan in a Greek olive grove.

Bottom left: Brigadier Puttick, who led the New Zealand Division in Crete. Three paintings by Captain Peter McIntyre, made at the time in Crete and Egypt.

Bottom right: A Maori soldier — one of the 28th New Zealand Battalion.

Below: The Kiwi — a typical New Zealand soldier.
/Illustrated London News

had won the Victoria Cross in World War 1 as a Lance Corporal, leading his section against two machine gun posts near Messines, destroying a third with the help of one other man and going on to clear a strong-point in a cellar. Tall, lean, black-moustached and a strict disciplinarian, he had trained his men well, but his orthodox outlook on soldiering were to be of little use to him in the next 48 hours. He now deployed his companies to defend the airfield and Hill 107 to the south of the main road. C Company was on the airfield itself with Lieutenant Sinclair's 15 Platoon on the west, dug in behind barbed wire along the bank of the dried up bed of the Tavronitis river; 13 Platoon on the seaward side and 14 Platoon with Captain Johnson's company headquarters just south of the main road. A Company commanded by Captain Hanton was behind them, holding the north side of Hill 107, with Captain Crarer's B Company on the southern extremity of the hill. D Company, Captain Campbell, was in position on the west side of the hill with Sergeant Sargeson's 18 Platoon covering the road bridge; 17 Platoon on the south-west foot of Hill 107; and 16 Platoon in between them and higher up the slope. Their trenches were dug beneath the olive trees and they covered the ground between the irrigation canal and the dry river-bed. Half a mile to the south on the edge of the river bed was a platoon outpost from the 21st Battalion, led by Lieutenant Anderson.

There were two machine gun platoons under Lieutenant Colonel Andrew's command from the 27th MG Battalion. 2/Lieutenant Brant, who was later wounded, had a section of two guns in D Company, covering the bridge and the river-bed and a section on top of the hill, firing over the airfield. The other platoon, led by Lieutenant Luxford, had a section on the eastern edge of the airfield covering the airfield and the beach and a second one on a spur above Maleme village. There were only seven belts, each of 250 rounds, available for each gun, enough for seven minutes' rapid fire. The two mortars were in a gully on the east of Hill 107, not far from battalion headquarters, and in Pirgos village were the three officers and 60 men of Headquarters Company.

The New Zealanders needed no urging to dig after their experience in Greece and they concealed their trenches and weapon pits with skill and care. Their Colonel put the finishing touches by flying over his battalion area to check how they looked from the air and all this effort paid a rich dividend in battle. On the airfield the round, sandbag gun-pits of the Bofors guns stood out clearly, both to the eye and on the German air photographs, as did the aircraft pens and the RAF tented camp. Yet the German pilots and their cameras saw very few of the New Zealand positions, either on Hill 107 or in the 23rd Battalion's area to the east.

On 14 May two Matilda tanks of B Squadron 7th Royal Tank Regiment arrived and went into a hide on the north side of Hill 107 above Maleme village, ready to counter-attack the airfield. These Matildas were armed with a 2-pounder gun and a 7.92mm Besa machine gun. They had a crew of four, weighed 26½ tons and could do 15mph. Although already outdated for tank v. tank

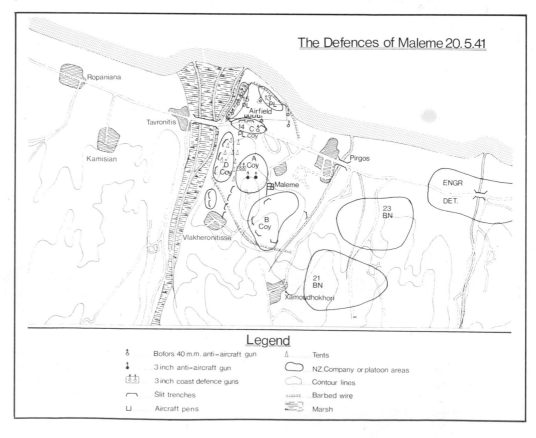

The Defences of Maleme 20.5.41

Legend

- ⌀   Bofors 40 m.m. anti-aircraft gun
- ⚫   3 inch anti-aircraft gun
- ⚬⚬   3 inch coast defence guns
- ⌣   Slit trenches
- ⊔   Aircraft pens
- △   Tents
- ⬭   NZ.Company or platoon areas
- ⌒   Contour lines
- ⌇⌇⌇   Barbed wire
- ▨   Marsh

fighting, they were usually reliable and were still useful against infantry in the open or in houses. Like much of the British equipment on Crete, these tanks were old and worn.

Maleme airfield had been a Royal Navy Fleet Air Arm station. Swordfish, Buffalos, Fulmars and a Gladiator had all operated from Maleme against the Italian Fleet and in an attempt to hold the rapidly increasing German air attacks. The Buffalos had long been unserviceable and were by now shot to ribbons anyway; the last Fulmar had been destroyed on the ground and the surviving Gladiator had somersaulted on take-off across the rough, sandy and bomb-scarred airfield. There were still 50 naval ground staff under Commander Beale in a camp near Maleme village and Lieutenant Sutton with 100 Cretans had worked hard to improve the defences by digging trenches, building aircraft pens and a command post and putting up barbed wire.

Maleme was also an RAF base and 30 Squadron's Mark I Blenheims had only left for Egypt in mid-April. About 100 of their ground crews were still at Maleme in a tented camp with two or three huts just south of the main road on the river side of Hill 107. Up to 19 May there had also been eight Hurricanes of 33 Squadron on the airfield, flown by any available pilots, including some from 80 Squadron and some from the Navy. Squadron Leader Howell, Sergeants Ripsher and Reynish and the other pilots had done wonders against overwhelming odds and it is surprising that any of them survived, as they daily flew three and four Hurricanes against hundreds of Me109 and 110s. Finally on 19 May the last Hurricane was ordered back to Egypt, leaving Squadron Leader Howell and 133 men from 33 Squadron in the RAF camp. They had a few rifles, revolvers and Italian carbines and set up three Lewis gun positions fortified with petrol cans filled with earth, one near the aircraft pens and two more in D Company area on Hill 107. One airman, Ginger Stone, fixed up a twin Browning machine gun mounting near the pens and another, Marcel Comeau, did the same with a Vickers K gun. Much of the airfield was obstructed with 50 gallon drums filled with 100-octane petrol and, if gliders landed, the Lewis guns were to set them alight with bursts of tracer.

Sited half way up the north west face of Hill 107 in a concrete blockhouse were two 4-inch coast defence guns manned by 'Z' Coast Defence Battery, Royal Marines and on 15 May a troop of 'C' Heavy Anti-Aircraft Battery, Royal Marines arrived with two 3-inch AA guns. Eight Bofors 40mm light AA guns also arrived manned by a troop of the Australian 7th Light AA Battery and another troop of the British 156 Light AA Battery. The eight Bofors were deployed round the airfield perimeter in sandbag emplacements, fully exposed to view, but with dummy gun positions interspersed among them, while the two 3-inch guns were dragged up to the top of Hill 107. The New Zealanders' suggestion that the Bofors might be more effective if hidden in the olive groves and gulleys of Hill 107, was turned down by the British and Australian Gunners. The Marines remained under command of their Base Headquarters in Suda, the Navy and the Air Force were more or less on their own and none of them was under command of Andrews and the 22nd Battalion.

The only artillery available to Lieutenant Colonel Andrews and the defence of Maleme were four French and three Italian 75mm field guns and two British 3.7-inch pack howitzers. Captain Williams, who was later wounded and captured, commanded the 3.7s in the area of 21 Battalion; Lieutenant Cade in B Troop placed his Italian 75s in the 23 Battalion positions and Captain Snadden's C Troop of French 75s, without sights or instruments, were in a direct fire position near Modhion, further east. The observation posts and forward observing officers for A and B troops were on Hill 107, connected by a single field-telephone line to the guns. There were no radios.

So some 620 New Zealand infantry, about 290 RAF and RN ground staff, 100 marines and 100 gunners were the close garrison of Maleme airfield with two 4-inch coast defence guns, two 3-inch anti-aircraft guns, eight Bofors 40mm anti-aircraft guns, eight Vickers Machine guns, two 3-inch mortars and a variety of Bren and Lewis light machine guns, No 4 rifles, Italian carbines, Thompson sub-machine guns and revolvers. They were all under heavy and continuous air attack by day, they had survived a strenuous and depressing retreat and evacuation from Greece and in the case of the RN and RAF ground staff they had seen the aircraft, which they serviced, shot out of the sky. But for three weeks they had been able to get some sleep at nights, they had enjoyed the swimming and the wines and fruit and sunshine of Crete and they knew what was coming — to such an extent that the New Zealanders mocked their first German prisoners by asking them why they were an hour late. Two miles away from Maleme were two more New Zealand battalions, warned to be ready to counter-attack the airfield if necessary, and within 10 miles to the east were the rest of the New Zealand Division.

The D-Day forecast by British Intelligence 16 May, went by and the tension mounted all over Crete. At Maleme on the 19th the last Hurricane took off for Egypt and 40 Me109s made a determined effort to wipe out the Bofors guns, inflicting heavy damage and casualties. That night many of the airmen went up into the slit trenches, which they had dug in the New Zealand A and D Company areas.

Before dawn on 20 May the rest of the sailors and airmen went up the hill and at 6.30am joined with the New Zealanders in the normal morning routine of 'standing to'; washed, shaved, armed, equipped and ready for whatever the day might bring.

The Battle for Maleme Airfield

As the light improved, the men in their slit trenches round the airfield and on Hill 107 heard and saw the expected swarms of Me109 fighter aircraft, flying in from the sea. Seconds later each aircraft peeled off from the formation and dived on to the Bofors guns and the empty aircraft pens on the airfield, firing long bursts from their machine guns and cannon. The British and Australian gunners kept their Bofors guns firing throughout each attack, disappearing in a flurry of shell bursts and dust, and near the aircraft pens two airmen, Comeau and Eaton, who had been buried alive twice in previous bomb attacks, fired their Browning and Vickers K guns at each diving Messerschmitt. Then there was a lull and at 7.30am the British in their slit trenches stood down and many of the airmen set off down the hill to their camp and to breakfast. As they reached the tents at about 7.45, an unusually heavy air attack began. It was pattern bombing by Heinkels and Dorniers on the airfield and Hill 107, the bombs bursting in gusts of flame and throwing up tall pillars of black smoke. The bombers dropped their sticks across the whole area, and in amongst them were Me110 fighter

bombers attacking targets, wherever they could see them and scoring a direct hit on the coast defence guns. Marcel Comeau was caught in his tent, looking for his pipe, so grabbing his rifle he jumped into a near-by slit trench. Above him he heard the sound of rushing air, and looking up, he saw a glider sweep past him. Then crashing through the olive trees, a second glider came straight at him, skidded round, hit his tent and stopped. Its door opened and a dazed German soldier stumbled out. Comeau shot both him and a second man behind him, fired a third time into the dark door of the glider fuselage and then took off up the hill back to D Company. By now the din was terrific, as everyone fired at the tug aircraft, the gliders and the Germans, jumping and staggering out of them.

The Germans of Koch's 1st Battalion, crammed in their gliders and sweating in their heavy clothing, had sighted Crete at about 7.40. Escorting fighters zoomed and banked round them and an Me109 flew so close to Erich Schuster's glider in No 3 Company, that they rocked and bounced in its slipsteam. Small black puffs of smoke appeared around them as they

Below: An Me109 on the beach near Platanias, after being hit by a Bofors shell./*IWM*

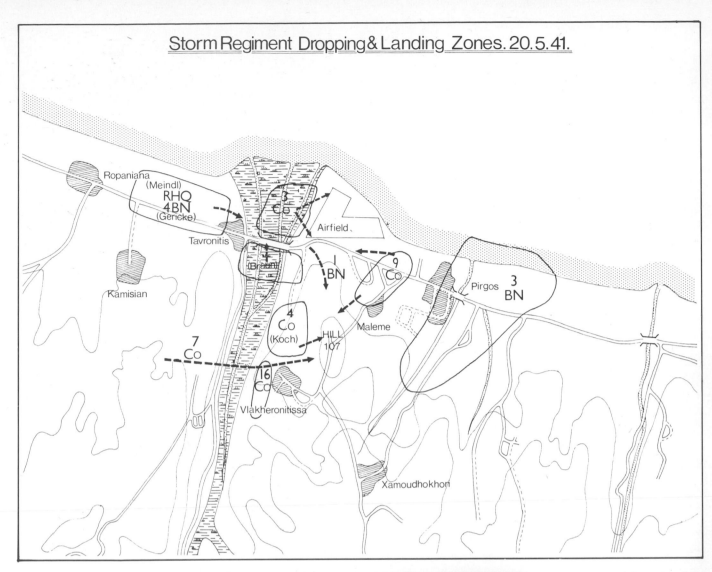

Storm Regiment Dropping & Landing Zones. 20.5.41.

Ropaniana

(Meindl)

RHQ
4BN
(Gericke)

Tavronitis

Kamisian

(Braun)

Airfield

I
BN

9
Co

Pirgos

3
BN

4
Co
(Koch)

HILL
107

Maleme

7
Co

16
Co

Vlakheronitissa

Xamoudhokhon

Left: A DFS 230 glider near Maleme — two men of the Sturmregiment pose for an 'action' shot.

came under British gunfire and then the gliders released from their tugs and dived down towards the airfield, the Ju52 transports banking away to the west and north for the long haul back to Greece for the second lift. As the gliders went down through heavy machine gun fire and the shells of the few Bofors guns still firing, the dive-bombers and fighters went with them, so that the gliders landed in the dust and smoke of the bomb-bursts and the impact of cannon shells and machine gun bullets. The three gliders of Oberfeldwebel Arpke's No 2 Platoon dived steeply to the river bed south of the road and then skimmed over the bridge to a landing among the boulders, close to the western edge of the airfield. The glider skids, wrapped in barbed wire to increase friction, scraped along the ground and then each glider stopped with a heavy, jolting lurch. Arpke's glider, still going very fast, hit a rock and burst open like a ripe melon. As the men scrambled out, they were met with the noise of battle — bomb-bursts, British rifles and machine guns firing as fast as they could, the crack and thump of bullets close to them and the continuous door-slamming tattoo of a British Bofors gun firing close in front of them.

Most of the men went to ground, but Schuster ran over to Arpke's smashed glider, as Arpke's

unconscious body was being lifted out. It looked like a fractured skull and beside him another man was having a broken arm set by the medical orderly. Schuster decided to take command of the platoon, ordered the injured man to stay with Arpke, collected the sections from the three gliders and gave out quick orders for an attack on the Bofors position in front of them. '1 Section right, 2 Section left, 3 Section covering fire — forward' and as he said it, an Me109 swooped down on the British gun position, pumping shells into it. Gefreiter Penzberger, just behind Schuster, was hit and fell dead, as a machine gun opened fire on them and the platoon took cover behind a fold in the ground. Schuster crawled forward to some bushes, until he could see the Bofors gun clearly and then signalled forward his machine gunner. They opened fire, but without much effect on the British gunners and the platoon stayed flat on their stomachs.

At a shout from one of his men, Schuster looked round to see his platoon commander, Arpke, running towards them in a series of short sprints. Collapsing beside Schuster, Arpke complained of a painful knee and a splitting headache, but in a few minutes had sized up the situation, moved the platoon back to the shelter of the river bed, organised machine gun and mortar covering fire and launched an attack on the anti-aircraft guns round the left flank. Schuster's section of six men led the attack, crawling through scrub-oaks and rocks until they got to within 30 metres of the British slit trenches. On a signal from Schuster, each man pulled the fuse of a grenade and hurled it into the enemy position. As the grenades exploded the seven

Germans ran forward. Schuster jumped into the trench, landed on a dead man, saw his first live enemy soldier two yards away and shot him with a burst from his Schmeisser. Firing as he went, he ran into the gun position. A man behind him threw a grenade, Schuster's machine carbine clicked empty, he flung himself down, re-loaded and, shouting to his section to cover him, dashed into the next trench and into some surprised British gunners. One of them fired at Schuster and missed and Schuster dodged back to his section. Now they could hear the sound of German machine carbines and grenades from the north where the other platoons were attacking the rest of the guns and the New Zealand 13 platoon near the shore. Their own mortar bombs began to burst on the next Bofors position and Schuster got his men up again and running forward. A bullet tore his sleeve and another creased his helmet, knocking him down. Up again, they checked for a moment to throw grenades into the half-roofed gun-pit and then they were all in it, firing at the gunners, killing, wounding and capturing the lot.

In the rest of 3 Company the commander, von Plessen, was killed in the attack on the guns, Leutnant Musyal had been badly wounded in the head ten metres from his glider, but Feldwebel Ellersiebe had led the platoon in a successful attack on the Bofors guns. Feldwebel Galla's section had been practically wiped out by Sinclair's 15 Platoon of the New Zealand C Company, firing from their trenches on the west perimeter of the airfield. In the third platoon Oberfeldwebel Scheel's tow-rope broke in flight, but they had landed safely on another island.

They rejoined the company four days later. His two other sections came down west of Tavronitis, fought through it, collected thirty prisoners, reached the company on the airfield and got one of the captured Bofors guns into action. Three gliders of 4 Company, led by Koch himself, landed amongst the tents of the RAF camp and six more on the western slopes of Hill 107 in the middle of the New Zealand 17 Platoon. They made a marvellous target for most of the New Zealand D Company and took heavy casualties. Major Koch was severely wounded in the head, the company commander, Hauptmann Sarrazin, was killed and the survivors dug in, where they were, on the lower slopes of the hill and kept up a continuous harassing fire against the New Zealanders above them. In the RAF camp there was some confused shooting and the few airmen amongst the tents were captured.

Major Braun's gliders made accurate landings, one of them stopping within ten metres of the west end of the bridge. As the men piled out, they came under intense machine gun fire from the New Zealand positions on Hill 107 and Braun was killed at once. His men succeeded in cutting the fuse-wires and removing the demolition charges under the bridge and were able to force Sergeant Sargeson's 18 Platoon back to the line of the irrigation canal, where he fought on all day, ending it with nine unwounded men.

Only 25 hectic minutes had gone by since the gliders landed at 8am. On the airfield the British and Australian gunners and New Zealand's C Company had been fighting furiously. On Hill 107 A and D Companies had been firing continuously at the gliders and the Germans in

Top left: German parachute soldiers in action with a Schmeisser machine carbine and an MG 34, their standard light machine gun in 1941./*IWM*

Bottom left: A German flamethrower in action, clearing a trench./*IWM*

Above: The main road bridge at Maleme. One of the DFS 230 gliders of Major Braun's bridge assault party. General Meindl was wounded in the dry river bed near the first pier.

Left: Emplaning for Crete./*IWM*

Below: Stand up! Hook up!/*IWM*

Bottom: The German technique of a diving exit./*IWM*

Top right: A German parachute soldier, jumping over Maleme, showing their technique of the dive forward, in contrast to the British and American 'feet first and feet together'.

Bottom right: Another view of a man dropping from a Ju52 over Crete on 20 May./*IWM*

the RAF camp on the lower slopes of Hill 107 and round the bridge, and the RAF and RN ground crews were fighting well as infantry from their trenches on Hill 107. A few of the keenest seekers after breakfast were dodging the Germans amongst the tents.

The Germans in 3 and 4 Companies and in Major Braun's bridge assault force had fought hard and had silenced the anti-aircraft guns on the west of the airfield, but they were considerably shaken by the strength and ferocity of their reception.

Now at half past eight the swelling roar of aircraft engines, greater and more continuous than the din of the previous air attacks, made them all look up to search the sky. Out of the south east, from inland and with the sun behind them came a great armada of Ju52 transports, flying in a close formation of vics of three aircraft above the men of the New Zealand 23rd and 22nd Battalions.

As the transports came down to their dropping height of 400 feet above the ground, the German parachute troops inside saw their own strike aircraft returning from their bomb and cannon attacks on Maleme airfield and Hill 107 and the aircrews and the Numbers 1 to jump, standing at the fuselage doors, could see the smoke rising from the bomb-bursts. In those last few seconds they were reassured by the sight of their supporting air strikes and the shock was all the greater, when they jumped into intense and accurate machine gun and rifle fire. The aircraft passed slowly overhead, the sticks of German parachute soldiers began jumping and from beyond the Tavronitis to east of Pirgos the sky filled with their brown, green and white parachutes. For the men on the ground it was a staggering sight and a marvellous target.

38

From all over Hill 107, from Maleme, Pirgos and the olive groves on the hill side, where the 23rd Battalion lay hidden, the rattle of machine gun and rifle fire swelled into a continuous roar. A Ju52 was hit and on its way down ploughed through a stick of parachutists hanging helplessly in their harnesses. Men could be seen landing in the sea, where the weight of their equipment took them down to a quick death. Major Stenzler's 2nd Battalion landed safely and accurately away to the west near Spilia and in an hour were assembled and ready for action. Leutnant Mürbe with eighty-one men from 6 Company at Kisamos Kastelli, five miles to the west, landed in two main groups north and south of the main road, east of the town, and were at once attacked by the 1st Greek Regiment with whom was their New Zealand adviser, Major Bedding. In a bitter fight the Germans were wiped out, losing 54 men killed and 28 as prisoners, of whom 20 were wounded, at a cost to the Greeks of 57 dead and 62 wounded. When the battle for Crete was over, the Germans complained that many of their dead had been mutilated, an accusation fiercely denied by the Greeks and Cretans. There is no doubt, however, about the ferocity of the Cretan resistance to the German invasion, of the shock this was to the German airborne troops and of the savagery of the subsequent reprisals.

Hauptmann Gericke's 4th Battalion dropped just north of Tavronitis village without many casualties, except for his 16 Company, which came down in the river bed to the south, as planned. Some of the battalion's mortars, machine guns and motor-cycles were damaged by heavy landings, but they had a good drop on the whole and were soon in their rendezvous near the village. Walter Gericke had jumped No 1 with General Meindl behind him as No 2. General Meindl had never done a parachute course and his only previous jump had been into action in Norway. At No 3 came the senior doctor in the regiment, Oberstarzt Dr Neumann, and both he and the general landed safely. Gericke's parachute was damaged by enemy fire and he made a fast, awkward landing, cutting his head and bruising an arm. Neumann set off to collect his medical team and set up shop in the village, while General Meindl went forward towards the bridge. The glider carrying the 200-watt rear-link radio, with Oberleutnant von Seelen and some signallers, smashed into rocks on landing, wrecking the radio and injuring von Seelen. The regiment's signal officer, Göttsche, succeeded in making contact with corps headquarters in Athens on a stand-by pack set, which had been dropped by parachute, and shortly afterwards he picked up Stenzler's 2nd Battalion and Gericke's 4th on a similar set. Meindl wanted to cross the bridge to find Koch and his 1st Battalion and to assess the situation, but the bridge was in full view of Hill 107 and any movement near it drew

Below: Ju52 carrying parachute troops of the Sturmregiment on the way to Crete./*IWM*

40

Right: The German parachute attack, 20 May. One Ju52 is hit and on fire. In the left foreground a gun comes down on a cluster of parachutes./*IWM*

Below: Another Ju52 on fire and going down./*IWM*

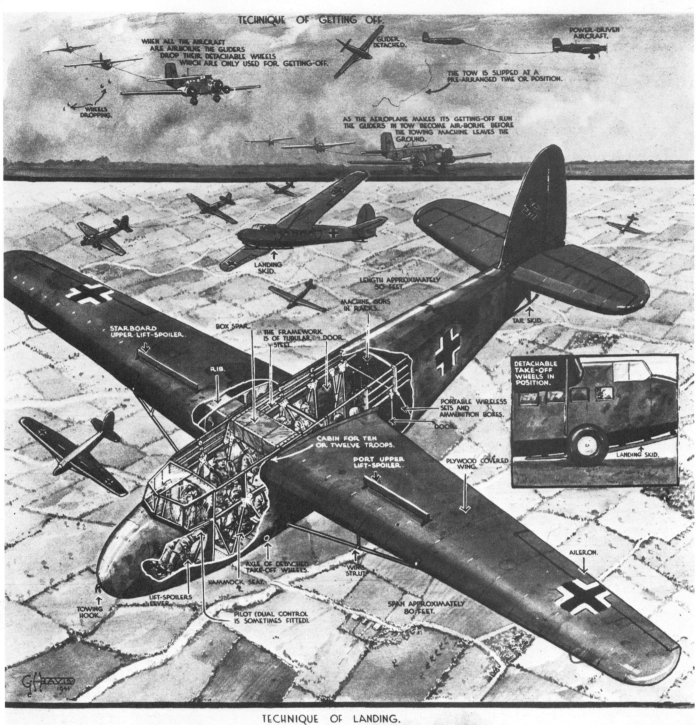

TECHNIQUE OF GETTING OFF.

WHEN ALL THE AIRCRAFT ARE AIRBORNE THE GLIDERS DROP THEIR DETACHABLE WHEELS WHICH ARE ONLY USED FOR GETTING-OFF.

GLIDER DETACHED.

POWER-DRIVEN AIRCRAFT.

THE TOW IS SLIPPED AT A PRE-ARRANGED TIME OR POSITION.

WHEELS DROPPING.

AS THE AEROPLANE MAKES ITS GETTING-OFF RUN THE GLIDERS IN TOW BECOME AIR-BORNE BEFORE THE TOWING MACHINE LEAVES THE GROUND.

STARBOARD UPPER-LIFT-SPOILER.

BOX SPAR.

THE FRAMEWORK IS OF TUBULAR STEEL.

DOOR.

LANDING SKID.

LENGTH APPROXIMATELY 50 FEET.

MACHINE GUNS IN RACKS.

TAIL SKID.

RIB.

PORTABLE WIRELESS SETS AND AMMUNITION BOXES.

DOOR.

CABIN FOR TEN OR TWELVE TROOPS.

PORT UPPER LIFT-SPOILER.

PLYWOOD COVERED WING.

DETACHABLE TAKE-OFF WHEELS IN POSITION.

LANDING SKID.

AILERON.

TOWING HOOK.

LIFT-SPOILERS LEVER.

HAMMOCK SEAT.

AXLE OF DETACHED TAKE-OFF WHEELS.

PILOT (DUAL CONTROL IS SOMETIMES FITTED).

WING STRUT.

SPAN APPROXIMATELY 80 FEET.

TECHNIQUE OF LANDING.

(1) GLIDER COMING IN TO LAND.

(2) GLIDER HELD LEVEL, TWO OR THREE FEET OFF THE GROUND.

(3) TAIL COMING DOWN GRADUALLY.—SKID ABOUT 12 INCHES OFF THE GROUND.

(4) GLIDER LANDED. IT REQUIRES ONLY ABOUT 12 YARDS TO DRAW UP.

36 FT.

Above: First attempts to explain how the Germans landed, published by the *Illustrated London News* in May 1941.

Right: More explanatory pictures from the *Illustrated London News* of July 1941, based on the Crete landings./*Illustrated London News*

42

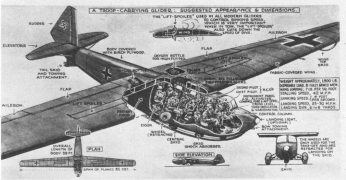

CARRIED FOR DISTANCES OF OVER 200 MILES ACROSS SEA, THOUSANDS OF GERMAN AIR-BORNE TROOPS INVADE CRETE: SKETCHES EXPLAINING ENEMY METHODS EMPLOYED IN LANDING, AND CONSOLIDATING POSITIONS.

Above: A typical, hastily dug weapon pit. The man asleep on the left has a sniper's rifle beside him with a telescopic sight and the sentry, fieldglasses slung round his neck and a stick grenade, ready on the parapet.

intense machine gun fire. Several parachutists who tried to cross in front of Meindl were killed, so Meindl ran down into the dry river bed and started to dodge across from pillar to pillar of the bridge. Gericke saw him fall, as a burst of fire hit him in the chest and two men ran out to bring him back into cover. He was taken to Neumann's dressing station in Tavronitis village, where it was at once realised that the General's best hope of survival lay in an immediate flight to Athens, a major operation and intensive care. Meindl himself remained fully conscious and insisted on retaining command of his regiment from the stretcher on which he lay in the village. In the few minutes at the bridge he had seen at once how Hill 107 dominated the airfield, and how essential it was to capture it, before the aircraft could land with the 5th Mountain Division, the all-important follow-up force.

Most of the German 3rd Parachute Battalion dropped into the middle of the New Zealand 23rd Battalion one and a half miles east of the airfield. The New Zealanders were dug in among the olive trees on a series of terraced ridges overlooking the main road and the coastal plain. As the German parachute soldiers neared the ground, they opened fire with their Schmeisser machine carbines at the enemy below, but they could do little to save themselves. Every rifle and Bren gun from the New Zealand slit trenches began firing at the parachutists hanging in their harness at the end of their rigging lines and, as they hit the ground, the New Zealanders leaped from their trenches and rushed to shoot, bayonet and club them, as they struggled to get free from their harness. Many of the 3rd Battalion were dead before they reached the ground, others were killed as they hung in the olive trees, and only a few reached their weapons' containers to fight back

bravely. Most of Leutnant Witzig's No 9 Company dropped near Maleme village between the 22nd and 23rd Battalions and so survived, but the rest of the 3rd Battalion were destroyed. Their commanding officer, Major Scherber, his adjutant, his intelligence officer, their doctor, three out of four company commanders and 400 men out of the 600 who had jumped were dead within ten minutes of jumping from their aircraft.

The men of the New Zealand 23rd Battalion were elated. They had won a victory and knew now that the German airborne attack must fail. The German dead lay all round them in hundreds. The Adjutant, sitting in an olive grove, had shot two without getting up from his packing-case desk and in Pirgos village Lieutenant Beaven and the 22nd Battalion's headquarters company had had a similar sort of field day.

At 9am Colonel Andrews at the 22nd Battalion headquarters decided to visit his companies to see what was happening, but the fire from the survivors of Koch's 4 Company near the RAF camp and in the river bed prevented him reaching D Company or C Company and the remants of the German 9 Company, south of Pirgos, stopped him getting to his own headquarters company. Radio contact with the New Zealand 5th Brigade at Platanias now failed and Andrew began to feel a little isolated. On seeing the gliders and parachutists land, Squadron Leader Howell and Commander Beale had gone down into the RAF camp to recover the confidential code books and to bring back to Hill 107 the airmen and sailors, who had gone in search of breakfast. Both Howell and Beale were wounded severely by men of Leutnant Kahless's platoon of Koch's battalion and at about 11am the clearance of the RAF

Above: A German MG 34 team in
action. The gun is on a tripod
mounting here, for sustained fire.
The No 1 or Corporal is watching
for a target and below him are
ammunition-belt boxes.

camp was completed by Oberleutnant Trebes,
with a few men of regimental headquarters and a
platoon from 3 Company. They captured some
30 airmen and a little later some of these RAF
prisoners were sent across the airfield to tell the
New Zealand C Company to surrender. In the
resulting exchange of fire a number of them were
killed, before the survivors were rescued by a
counter-attack led by Pilot Officer Wheaton,
which also inflicted casualties on the Germans
near the bridge.

For the rest of the day small groups of the
German 1st Battalion and of regimental
headquarters held on to their positions in the
RAF camp and in the river bed. Although pinned
down there by fire from the New Zealand
D Company and in particular from Sergeant
Sargeson's platoon in the irrigation canal near the
bridge, these few Germans were able to prevent
free movement on Hill 107 above them and to
exercise a considerable influence on Lieutenant
Colonel Andrew and his growing sense of
isolation.

On the west edge of the airfield 15 Platoon of
C Company had taken the full weight of attack
by von Plessen's 3 Company, but were still alive
and in action. They had lost a lot of men, their
platoon commander, Lieutenant Sinclair was
wounded painfully in the neck and his batman
Private Farrington had been shot through the
head. Sinclair persisted with grenades in trying to
set fire to the fuel-filled drums on the airfield and
his platoon held their positions until nightfall.
When one of Erich Schuster's grenades landed in
a 15 Platoon trench, Lance Corporal McHaffey
banged his steelhelmet over it and stood on the
helmet as the grenade exploded. Both his
feet were blown off and he died an hour
later.

This New Zealand Company's main enemy, 3
Company of the German 1st Battalion, had lost
their initial impetus by 10am. They had silenced
four Bofors guns on the western perimeter, but
their company commander von Plessen was dead
and the only other officer, Leutnant Musyal, was
badly wounded. The company medical officer, Dr
Weizel, had set up his aid post in a captured
British tent pitched in the river bed near the
bridge and together with his orderly, Gefreiter
Müller, had got most of the wounded back there
or to Dr Neumann's main dressing station in
Tavronitis. Weizel now assumed command of the
company, reorganised them into a proper
defensive position and generally took hold of their
situation and their spirits.

At 11am he sent off one of his platoons to help
Trebes clear the RAF camp site, south of the
bridge and then at 1215pm Oberleutnant Dobke
reported to him with 15 men from the 4th
Battalion with orders from regiment to attack and
clear the enemy from the north end of the airfield
near the shore. This was the area held by the New
Zealand 13 Platoon, who had so far had a
successful morning, shooting up the German
3 Company.

Just after Dobke's party had left 3 Company
headquarters, a message arrived to say that an air
attack was about to go in on Dobke's objective.
Weizel sent a man running after him, but the
warning never reached him and Dobke and his
men were not seen again. They were all killed by
13 Platoon, who continued to hold their positions
without much difficulty until after dark that
evening.

The Germans in 3 Company spent the rest of
the morning improving their position and
exchanging fire with the New Zealand platoons of
C Company. They had lost 17 men killed, 19

badly wounded and eight more lightly wounded, who stayed with the company. They were all hot and tired and Erich Schuster took off his woollen jersey and cut off his long trouser legs. Their rations of spiced brown bread, chocolate, rusks, sugar and cigarettes melted together into an unappetising mess and they were short of water. They felt better when one of the men, Kurze, brought a jar of wine back from Tavronitis, but the news of General Meindl's wound depressed them and they all expected a furious British counter-attack at any time.

At 10.55am wireless contact between the New Zealand 22nd Battalion and 5th Brigade was re-established and Lieutenant Colonel Andrews reported to Brigadier Hargest that he was being heavily attacked. An hour later Lieutenant Colonel Leckie came up on the air from the 23rd Battalion, telling his brigadier that the situation in his area was in complete control. He had in fact only lost seven men killed and 30 wounded and his battalion were in high spirits after their morning victory.

Across the river in Tavronitis village General Meindl, lying on his stretcher, had heard nothing

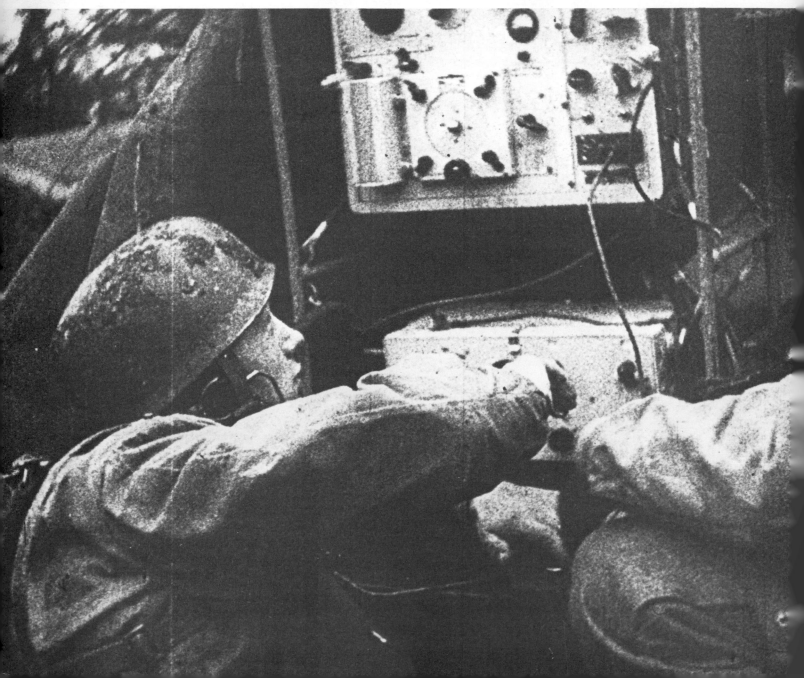

from the 3rd Battalion and he was beginning to realise that they must be in trouble. His 1st Battalion had taken heavy losses and were held up on the airfield and below Hill 107 and although the 4th Battalion mortars and heavy machine guns were in action, their only infantry, the pioneer company, was a mile away guarding the southern flank.

Major Stenzler's 2nd Battalion was more or less complete and ready for action except for Leutnant Mürbe's 80 men, five miles to the west at Kastelli, from whom nothing had been heard. All but 28 of them were already dead.

At 1pm Meindl ordered Stenzler to send two companies round the southern flank of Hill 107 to attack the New Zealand positions from the rear. Oberleutnant Barmetler moved off at 1.30 with 7 and 8 Companies on a long, fast and sweaty approach march over the hills. At Vlakheronitissa they were held up by fire from a platoon outpost from the 21st New Zealand battalion in the Tavronitis river bed below the village, and after by-passing them the German companies were stopped on the lower slopes of Hill 107 by fire from the 22nd Battalion's B Company and by some accurate shooting by the 75mm guns of 27 Battery. Ju87 dive bombers and Gericke's mortars pounded the top of Hill 107 in support of Barmetler's advance to such effect that at 3.50 Andrew withdrew his battalion headquarters from the top of the hill to B Company's position at the southern end of the 107 feature. Just before 3 o'clock he had also radioed to brigade that his 'headquarters were penetrated', but it is not clear by whom. There is no record of any German claim to have got that far. At the same time Andrew ordered that the flares be sent up, which were to call for a counter-attack on Hill 107 by

the 23rd Battalion, but they were not seen by anyone at Leckie's headquarters.

Although the German machine guns and mortars were active all the afternoon, the only significant German movement had been the approach of Stenzler's two companies from the south-west, but the combination of this fire and movement with Andrew's lack of communication with his C, D and HQ Companies made him ask brigade urgently at 5pm for a counter-attack from the 23rd Battalion.

With plenty of daylight left, some British artillery still firing effectively with observation from Hill 107, with the hindsight of the German casualties and exhaustion and the comparative solidity of the New Zealand C and D Companies, it is now clear that a counter-attack by the 850 men of the 23rd and 21st Battalions carried right across the Tavronitis river would have destroyed General Meindl's Storm Regiment. This would have denied Maleme airfield to any subsequent landings and so ensured the failure of the whole assault.

From his headquarters at Platanias Brigadier Hargest told Andrews by telephone that the 23rd Battalion could not come to his aid as 'they were engaged with parachute troops', an inexplicable reply in the light of Colonel Leckie's cheerful reports. So Andrews decided to mount his own counter-attack and ordered Captain Johnson in C Company to organise it. Lieutenant Donald's 40 men of 14 Platoon, the two Matilda tanks and an officer and 15 men from 156 Light Anti-Aircraft Battery, who had specially asked to be allowed to join in, made up the attacking force and their objective was the road bridge over the river.

They moved out at 5.15 astride the main road with the infantry spread out each side of the two

Top left: Another picture of men of the Sturmregiment, waiting to attack Platanias after they had advanced east from Maleme.

Bottom left: Two signallers near Tavronitis trying to raise corps headquarters in Athens./*IWM*

Above: Dr Neumann, with his back to the camera, watching British and New Zealand prisoners coming up Hill 107 on the morning of 21 May — probably a mixture of the New Zealand D Company and RAF and RN men from the airfield camp.

47

Right: One of the two Matilda tanks from 7th Royal Tank Regiment which counter-attacked the main road bridge on 20 May with Lieutenant Donald's platoon of C Company. The German soldier looking at it is wearing the solar topee issued to each man, but seldom worn, and what look like British shorts.

tanks and advanced towards the bridge. Almost at once they came under intense fire from the German of Braun's party, from a few men of 4 Company round the bridge and from Dr Weizel's 3 Company to the north of it. As the tanks neared the bridge, several of the German parachutists there lost their heads and ran for it and the word spread rapidly among 3 Company that 'tanks were coming'. In one tank the ammunition would not fit the gun and the tank stopped on the road short of the bridge. The second tank pushed on boldly to the bridge and down the steep slope to the river bed, firing at the Germans and causing a considerable rout amongst them.

Erich Schuster's section in the river bed north of the bridge heard the noise of tank tracks and saw the khaki shirts and flat helmets of Donald's party advancing along the road. Schuster's machine gunner, Sieboldt, opened fire and attracted the attention of the leading tank. A two-pounder shell knocked down a tree behind them and a second shell burst on the lip of their trench but did no harm to Schuster and Sieboldt crouching in the bottom. As the tank drove under the bridge and turned north down the dry river bed, three or four German machine guns opened fire on its vision-slits, two mortar bombs scored direct hits with a noise like a cracked bell and a 37mm anti-tank gun loosed off several rounds from Tavronitis village. A few yards further on the tank stopped amid the boulders and its crew climbed out to surrender. Only three of Donald's platoon got back to C Company unwounded and the gunner officer with him was killed. Lieutenant Donald himself was wounded, but survived, to be wounded three more times before the end of the war and to win the DSO and MC

Although a costly failure, this small counter-attack had a considerable effect on the Storm Regiment. Almost as soon as the two Matilda tanks appeared on the road, heading for the bridge, a message was sent off from General Meindl's headquarters in Tavronitis to the XI Air Corps in Athens on Göttsche's radio saying 'enemy tanks attacking from Maleme are coming over the airfield. Their attack halted for the moment. Drop of anti-tank ammunition urgently required on the beach one kilometre west of the bridge'. General Meindl was now weak from loss of blood and it was becoming urgent to get him back to Athens for proper surgery. Gericke and Stenzler had together taken over effective command at regimental headquarters; the remnants of Koch's two glider companies were dug in north and south of the bridge and the 1st Battalion's doctor, Neumann, had taken over command of the battalion. The mortars and machine guns of Gericke's IV Battalion were in action in the Tavronitis river bed and round Tavronitis village, but they were running short of ammunition. Leutnant Barmettler's attack on the south west slopes of Hill 107 with 7 and 8 Companies of the 2nd Battalion had been halted short of Vlakheronitissa. News of the destruction of Scherber's 3rd Battalion had by now been brought in by survivors of 9 Company.

There were only about 650 unwounded German soldiers left out of the 2,300 who had landed that morning. The were all tired and thirsty, and ammunition was running low. Every man of them expected a heavy British counter-attack at first light next morning or sooner and most of them, including Erich Schuster in his slit trench on the Western edge of the airfield, Hauptmann Gericke at regimental headquarters and General Meindl on his stretcher, realised that no reinforcing troop carriers could land, until Hill 107 was cleared of the enemy. The Storm Regiment's situation report to XI Air Corps that evening ended with the words 'without reinforcements the attack on Crete cannot succeed'.

In Athens General Student had received a series of gloomy messages all day. The 7th Division's commander, General Süssmann, had been killed in a glider crash on the island of Aegina. Both wings of his glider had broken off in the turbulence caused by a Heinkel III, passing close to their tug/glider combination. Von Heidrich's 3rd Parachute Regiment had taken heavy casualties and were making no progress towards Canea and Suda Bay. Oberst Bräuer's 1st Parachute Regiment, dropping between 4pm and 6.30pm at Heraklion into the murderous fire of the defending British battalions, had lost 1,000 men in the first half-hour. There was no contact with Rethymnon, but here in fact the 2nd Parachute Regiment were fighting for their lives against the vigorous attacks of Lieutenant Colonel Campbell's two Australian battalions.

General Student sat at his table in his command post, a room in the Hotel Grande Bretagne, through most of the day and night. A map of Crete on the wall carried paper flags showing the British and German positions and on a brightly lit table in the centre were field telephones, files and papers. After the war he wrote:

'In spite of much misgiving and doubt, I now had to decide to concentrate all my strength in one place in order to secure an airfield as soon as possible. My choice fell on Maleme.'

Here the Storm Regiment had made more progress than the parachute regiments at Canea, Rethymnon and Heraklion, and Maleme lay closest to the take-off airfields in Greece. The VIII Air Corps were to give their maximum effort to the support of the Storm Regiment at Maleme. Two companies from the 2nd Battalion, 2nd Parachute Regiment, who had not been able to take off for Heraklion, were available as a reserve and to these men could be added another two companies of individual sticks of parachutists, left behind on other airfields. This force was now ordered to drop at Maleme on the next day, 21 May. Student also told Hauptmann Kleye, an enterprising pilot on his staff, to try to land a Ju52 at Maleme as soon as possible to find out what was happening. Kleye took off at 3am and at first light touched down at the far end of the airfield near the beach to find that the artillery and small arms fire on the airfield seemed to be less. There was no real news of what the enemy were doing, but he was able to take General Meindl and some other wounded men back to Athens. Not long after he had taken off again, six more Ju52s landed on the beach near Spilia bringing much needed mortar and machine gun ammunition.

At 5.45pm Captain Johnson told 22nd Battalion headquarters that the counter-attack had failed, that 15 Platoon on the western edge of the airfield had been overrun and that 14 near the road was very weak. There was no news at battalion headquarters from D or HQ Companies and Andrews had not been able to visit either company. A stray soldier from D Company told Andrews, quite wrongly, that the whole of D Company were killed or prisoners, a typical example of the urge to bear ill tidings in self-excuse. Andrew's courage was never in question, but his inactivity on this vital day remains a mystery. Between him and his headquarters company in Pirgos there were certainly Germans, survivors of the 3rd Battalion's 9 Company, but his A, D and B Companies were only two to three hundred yards away with plenty of covered ways to them. Squadron Leader Howell and Commander Beale moved freely about Hill 107, until they were wounded, as did Marcel Comeau and other airmen. Comeau himself visited all three of the New Zealand companies round Hill 107 during the morning.

Standing on Hill 107 today with the advantage of knowing the situation of both sides and making every allowance for the air supremacy of the German Air Force and the threat of a seaborne landing, it is still difficult to understand why

Below: Maleme — one Ju52 lands past another on fire./*IWM*

Above: An Me110 attempts to land at Maleme past wrecked Ju52./*IWM*

Top right: The Sturmregiment bring into action one of the Bofors 40mm guns captured on Maleme airfield./*IWM*

Bottom right: Men of the mountain division on their march round the southern flank./*IWM*

Andrew never went to his companies to see for himself; why Brigadier Hargest never came forward to assess the situation; and why the 23rd and 21st Battalions were not launched into a counter-attack on that first day. They were first-rate fighting soldiers, fit, rested and full of confidence after their slaughter of the Storm Regiment's 3rd Battalion that morning. They would have annihilated the tired, thirsty survivors of the Storm Regiment. They too were good soldiers, but there were only 600 of them still on their feet. By denying to General Student the use of Maleme airfield, Andrew and Hargest might have initiated the ultimate defeat of the whole XI Air Corps assault.

At 6pm Andrew radioed to Brigadier Hargest that he must withdraw unless reinforcement reached him soon. The Brigadier replied 'if you must, you must.' Five minutes later another message from brigade told Andrew that a company from the 28th Maori Battalion and another from the 23rd were to be sent up in support of the 22nd. At 7pm the Maori company started off from Platanias on their long march.

By 9pm these two companies had not yet reached the 22nd Battalion and Andrew ordered a withdrawal to the B Company positions on the south end of Hill 107. Half an hour later the company from the 23rd reached Hill 107 and occupied the positions just vacated by the 22nd's A Company. There was still no sign of the Maori company. At 10pm Andrew decided that C, D and HQ Companies, together with the newly

arrived company from the 23rd, should withdraw to the area held by the 23rd and 21st Battalions. At midnight they began to move and soon the top of Hill 107 was empty of men and weapons.

Down on the western slope of the hill Captain Campbell still had 46 men of his own D Company and 60 airmen and marines. Sergeant Sargeson and his eight men held their position in the irrigation canal, overlooking the RAF camp and the bridge, and the whole of D Company were in good spirits. C Company were still holding the south and east sides of the airfield with their remaining two platoons and in Pirgos HQ Company had only lost Sergeant Matheson killed and five men wounded in a day of splendid shooting at the unfortunate Germans of the 3rd Battalion.

At 1.30am the Maori company passed through Pirgos, never saw the 22nd's HQ Company, went up on to Hill 107, found it empty and eventually bumped into Colonel Andrew near Xamoudkhokhori. They then walked the long road back to their battalion, killing some 40 stray Germans on the way.

Captain Campbell from D Company at about this time went up to Hill 107 to speak to his colonel and found no one there. Thinking rightly that he was now very isolated, he sent off Sergeant Sargeson with his eight men and all the walking wounded to make their way to the south coast. This they succeeded in doing and arrived at Sphakia four days later in time to be evacuated. Captain Craig and 17 Platoon were captured by

Gericke's men next morning, but Craig proved difficult to hold and escaped twice from prisoner of war camps. Campbell and the rest of his company together with most of the airmen managed to rejoin the 22nd Battalion next day in their new positions near the 23rd Battalion. At 3am HQ Company withdrew from Pirgos and at 4am Captain Johnson from C Company also climbed Hill 107 in search of battalion headquarters. He tried in vain to find the other companies and as German patrols were by now moving round behind his positions, he led his 50 unwounded men, carrying most of their wounded with them, up through A and B Companies' old positions and so back to the 23rd Battalion. By 4 o'clock in the morning there was no one left in the old 22nd Battalion positions and Hill 107, the key to Maleme airfield, was empty.

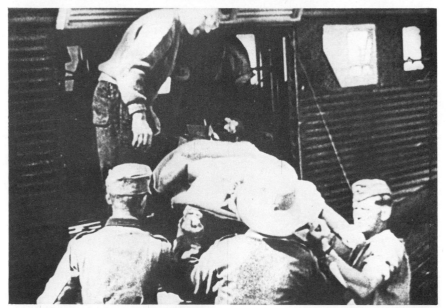

Through this same night the Germans of Koch's 1st Battalion, of Braun's assault platoon, of Gericke's 4th Battalion and of Stenzler's 2nd Battalion clung to their positions round the western and south western base of Hill 107, at the bridge and on the western edge of the airfield and their double sentries peered into the night, expecting to hear at any moment the sound of the enemy advancing to sweep them off their positions in the all-out counter-attack, which every German soldier believed was bound to come. South of the bridge, in the RAF camp and on the lower slopes of Hill 107, leadership was scarce. Braun was dead, Koch badly wounded and Barmetler's two companies of the 2nd Battalion near Vlakeronitissa were exhausted after their long day of marching and fighting. Dr Neumann had taken over command of the mixed

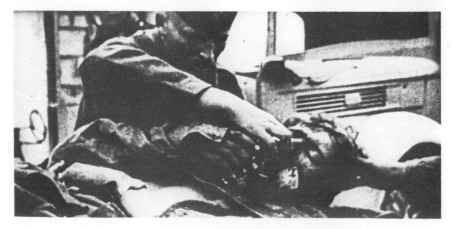

group of 1st and 4th Battalion men south of the bridge and Dr Weizel was leading 3 Company north of it. One of the few surviving officers, Oberleutnant Trebes, was helping Weizel and it was from 3 Company that the only patrols went out during the night. Erich Schuster led one of them, himself and three men, and got as far as the eastern edge of the airfield, where they threw grenades into one of C Company's section positions.

At the Storm Regiment headquarters in Tavronitis village Gericke had seen General Meindl loaded into Kleye's aircraft in the early morning and soon afterwards, at about 4.30am, he received a radio message from General Student ordering him to capture and clear the airfield at all cost and telling him that two fresh parachute companies would land at 2pm west of the airfield, and two more at 2.30pm east of Maleme village. He was to mount an attack on the airfield from both west and east.

On hearing this news Dr Neumann in the 1st Battalion and Barmetler in the 2nd sent patrols forward to feel their way cautiously up Hill 107 in the early morning twilight, which they were astonished to find abandoned. At the same time some of Gericke's 4th Battalion and Dr Weizel's 3 Company pushed forwards into the western outskirts of Maleme village, where they were halted by rifle and machine gun fire from some of the houses. Since the New Zealanders of C Company had retreated some time earlier, this shooting must have come from New Zealand stragglers or Cretans in the village. At about 8.30am some Ju52s came over and dropped 300 men west of the river bed, who were sent to

reinforce the 1st and 4th Battalion groups. As they crossed the bridge, they were fired on from the olive trees near the old RAF camp. A section ran forward and captured a lone New Zealander, Sergeant John Woods, who had chosen to stay behind and hunt the enemy rather than withdraw with his company.

Down on the airfield 3 Company got a British Bofors gun into action and on Hill 107 the men of 5 Company had manned a British 3-inch anti-aircraft gun. Both guns were trying to knock out the British artillery, which was still firing on to the airfield from the 23rd and 21st Battalion positions. Without observation posts on Hill 107 and with only 75mm guns they could do little real damage, but their shells continued to harass the Germans and to affect their minds powerfully for another twelve hours.

At 3pm dive-bombers and fighters put in an exceptionally heavy attack on Maleme and Pirgos and on the 23rd Battalion in their olive groves overlooking Pirgos. At the same time another close formation of Ju52s droned in from the sea and began dropping parachutists along the coastal plain between Pirgos and Platanias, right under the machine guns and rifles of the New Zealand Engineers and the Maori Battalion.

The men dropping were the 5th and 6th Companies of the 2nd Parachute Regiment, whose parent regiment was fighting hard at Rethymnon, and they were led by Leutnant Nagele. Their fate was much the same as Major Scherber's 3rd Battalion on the previous day. As they came down many of them were killed and wounded while still in the air and once the parachutists were on the ground, the New

Zealand sappers and the Maoris rushed to shoot and bayonet them. In minutes all the officers and NCO's of 5 Company were dead, together with most of their men, and Nagele was only able to collect 80 men in Pirgos village after dark that evening.

Seeing the Ju52s fly over and the air attacks going in ahead of his men, Gericke now pressed on through Maleme and into Pirgos. In a gully east of Hill 107 his men came on the regimental aid post of the New Zealand 22nd Battalion, full of New Zealand and German wounded in the care of Captain Longmore, the 22nd Battalion's medical officer. They had avoided attack by the German dive-bombers and fighters by laying out the wounded in a circle, on the instructions of the German prisoners. Meeting with no opposition in Pirgos, Gericke's men fanned out on each side of the road beyond the village in an attempt to continue their advance to silence those British guns. Here they met a withering fire from two companies of the New Zealand 23rd Battalion and drew back into the village leaving many dead and wounded behind them.

The Storm Regiment and their reinforcing companies now held Hill 107, Maleme and Pirgos. The British guns were still able to fire on to the airfield and some of the 23rd Battalion could see it and fire on it at extreme range with machine guns. But at 5pm the familiar, swelling roar of aircraft engines showed that General Student had launched the 5th Mountain Division. He was determined to pile into Maleme the reinforcements which were so essential, if they were to roll up the British defences from the west.

Sixty Ju52s flying in their usual vic formation began landing on Maleme airfield and as they did so, the nine British 75mm guns intensified their fire. As the first aircraft came to a halt at the end of the runway, the mountain troops jumped out and began to unload their rucksacks, weapons and motor-bikes, as fast as they could. Round the airfield perimeter and alongside the runway the men of Dr Weizel's 3 Company had prepared slit trenches and were ready to guide and help the newcomers. Erich Schuster stood up and waved his arm and the men from the first aircraft ran towards him. The second Junkers landed with its tail on fire and as it ran across the airfield, the doors opened and the men inside began jumping out and falling over. At the end of the runway it exploded. Another aircraft ran into a bomb crater and turned over, but the big, tri-motored planes kept on landing, dodging each other and the bomb craters, off-loading their men and stores and taking off again with the least possible delay.

The men of 3 Company helped where they could and hacked away with axes at another aircraft on fire, to free the men inside. This was the 2nd Battalion of the 100th Mountain Regiment and in forty-five minutes 650 men had landed safely on the airfield. Their Commanding officer, Major Friedmann, was badly wounded by a shellburst as he jumped from his aircraft and a

motor-cycle and sidecar raced over the airfield to pick him up. Six Ju52s chose the beach near Pirgos in preference to the airfield, now littered with 20 wrecked transports to add to the burned out Buffaloes and Hurricanes already there, but nearly all of these transports were hit by artillery, mortar and machine gun fire. Casualties to the men inside were surprisingly light and they were soon able to join the parachute troops in Pirgos. Before these first landings by the transport aircraft were complete, someone had started up a British bulldozer found on the airfield and had begun pushing the wrecked aircraft off the airfield. It was a triumph of determination and skilful flying and the arrival of this fresh battalion put new heart into the men of the Storm Regiment.

Half an hour later Oberst Ramcke with his new ADC, Leutnant Reil, dropped by parachute just north of Tavronitis village with orders from General Student to take command of the Western Group and to press on to the east to link up with Heidrich's 3rd Parachute Regiment. Bernhard-Hermann Ramcke had started his working life as a ship's boy. He was now fifty-two and had volunteered for parachute duties in the previous year. A year later, in 1942, he led the Ramcke Parachute Brigade against the British 8th Army and was wounded at El Alamein.

Top left: Captain Peter McIntyre's picture of 22nd Battalion's regimental aid post in a gully, just east of Hill 107, run by M.O. Captain Longmore and captured pm on 21 May. */Illustrated London News*

Bottom left: A Ju52 landing at Maleme./*IWM*

Above: Ju52 being unloaded on 21 May./*IWM*

Ramcke jumped in a combat jacket and riding boots, without the usual knee pads. He made a good landing, but was dismayed to see one of his aircraft dropping its stick into the sea. A few minutes later he met Leutnant Göttsche, the signals officer, who gave him a full report on what was happening; After a quick look at the airfield, the bridge and Hill 107, Ramcke summoned an order group made up of Hauptmann Gericke from the 4th Battalion, Major Stenzler from the 2nd, Oberst Utz from the 100th Mountain Regiment and the commander of the reinforcing parachute companies who had dropped that afternoon, Hauptmann Schmitz.

One company of the Mountain Regiment was sent to clear the Spatha peninsula to the north west, where the small ship flotilla carrying the 3rd Battalion of the 100th Mountain Regiment was due to land that night. Another company was given to Gericke to strengthen his hold on Maleme and Pirgos and to enable him to push on eastwards, and the rest of the battalion deployed to protect the airfield from the south and west. Later on they were to advance round the enemy's southern flank through the foothills once the rest of their regiment had landed. Ramcke was a vigorous and effective leader, well aware of the need to press on eastwards, but both he and Utz of the 100th Mountain Regiment felt that the battle might go either way. They had now some 1,500 men at Maleme, but they still expected at any minute a powerful British counter-attack, and they were amazed that they had not yet had to face one. In fact the New Zealand Division and 5th Brigade were planning one that same evening. The New Zealand 20th and 28th Maori Battalions were to attack along the main road, with the 20th on the right going for Maleme airfield and the 28th on the left with Hill 107 and the Tavronitis river as their objectives. Three light tanks of the 3rd Hussars were to lead the way along the road.

At 11.30 that night the troops on both sides saw gun-flashes to the north, away out to sea, and caught the rumble of distant gunfire. Eighteen miles north of Canea Force D of the Royal Navy's Mediterranean Fleet had met the German small ship flotilla, carrying the 3rd Battalion, 100th Mountain Regiment, heavy weapons for the Storm Regiment and part of the 2nd Parachute Anti-Aircraft Battalion. In two and a half hours the British cruisers and destroyers sunk a dozen caiques, two small steamers and a steam yacht and scattered the rest of the convoy. The lone Italian torpedo boat escort, Lupo, was hit eight times, but managed to pick up a good many men from the sea and the German Air Sea Rescue Service saved many more. Out of the 2,331 German mountain and parachute soldiers in the convoy, 324 were drowned including the battalion commander. Only 100 reached Crete in rubber boats without equipment or weapons.

At 10.10 next morning the Royal Navy's Force C came upon part of the second convoy

escorted by the Italian torpedo boat Sagittario. Sagittario and several caiques were hit, but the torpedo boat managed to lay a thick smoke screen behind which the caiques scattered. By these two actions the Royal Navy prevented any German reinforcements reaching Crete by sea, but at the cost from air attack that same day of two cruisers and a destroyer sunk and two battleships and two cruisers damaged.

By midnight on 22 May Lieutenant Colonel Dittmer's Maoris were on their startline just west of Platanias, but there was no sign of the 20th Battalion. At 2.45am two companies of the 20th arrived and the attack started. Both the Maoris and the 20th met small groups of German parachute troops in the villages and houses along their advance and it took some savage hand-to-hand fighting to clear them. These were survivors of the 3rd Battalion landing on the first day and of the two reinforcing companies dropped on the second day, and their continuing to hold out in their isolated positions delayed the New Zealand advance so much, that it was daylight by the time the attack reached Pirgos. C Company 20th Battalion were soon fighting Gericke's parachutists in Pirgos with bayonet, rifle, pistol and club and one of Leutnant Kiebitz's anti-tank guns, dropped at Maleme the day before, knocked out the leading light tank of the 3rd Hussars, setting it on fire and killing Sergeant Skedgewell, the tank commander, and his gunner and wounding the driver. Lieutenant Farran's tank lost a bogie and as the men of C Company emerged from Pirgos they made a good target for Major Stenzler's 2nd Parachute Battalion, now dug in on Hill 107. D Company of the New Zealand 20th reached the airfield, recaptured and destroyed two Bofors guns, but were then forced to withdraw by fire from Hill 107 and from all round them on the airfield.

The Maoris of the 28th Battalion overcame all resistance on their route forward by charging with the bayonet, shouting their deep-throated 'Ah! Ah!' and firing from the hip as they ran, but even their fighting spirit could not take them past Pirgos or overcome the fire from the machine guns and mortars of the German parachute soldiers on Hill 107 and in Maleme village.

A simultaneous attack by the 21st Battalion through Vlakheronitissa against the south-eastern slopes of Hill 107 was beaten back by the same intensity of fire and by late afternoon the New Zealand counter-attack had stopped and their battalions were consolidating on the line of the 23rd Battalion's position round Dhaskhaliana.

While this fierce and confused fighting was going on, Ju52 aircraft continued to land at Maleme all through the day. It was Ascension Day and under a light cloud cover the weather was fine and comparatively cool. An XI Air Corps airfield maintenance unit under Oberstleutnant Snowdazki had arrived and using British trucks and one of the Matilda tanks, worked all day to clear the airfield and its runway

of the British and German wrecks, which covered it. Twenty planes an hour landed, bringing in the 1st Battalion 85th Mountain Regiment between 10am and 12 noon and after them the 1st Battalion, 100th Mountain Regiment. Both battalions set off at once on their march round the south flank. The British 75mm guns, now in position near Modhion, were still shelling the airfield and caused some casualties to the two mountain battalions, in spite of continuous efforts by the dive bombers of the VIII Air Corps to find and destroy the guns.

At midday the Chief of Staff XI Air Corps, General Schlemm, arrived in a Ju52 to see the situation and to confirm Ramcke's orders. Group West, the Storm Regiment and the 5th Mountain Division, were to press on to the east and link up with Heidrich's 3rd Parachute Regiment. The VIII Air Corps would continue to support them, but for this day, 22 May, the Luftwaffe's task was to find and sink British warships in Cretan waters. General Student had been refused permission to move to Crete and the commander of the Mountain Division, General-major Ringel would arrive that evening and take over command of Group West.

At 3.50pm a field hospital unit landed and set up in Tavronitis village, taking over from Dr Neumann's main dressing station and a number of wounded were flown back to Greece in the returning transports. Then at 8pm General Ringel and his staff arrived and established a command post in Tavronitis. Shortly before him the

95th Mountain Engineer Battalion had landed, together with some of the mountain artillery and Major Bode's battery of parachute artillery. The German build-up at Maleme was properly under way and the real meaning of the loss to the British of Hill 107 and of command of the airfield was becoming clearer every hour.

Soon after he landed, Ringel summoned an order group and divided his force into three battle groups. Major Schätte's mountain engineers would be responsible for the close defence of the airfield and the clearance of Kastelli and Palaiokhora to the west. All the parachute units would form a second battle group under Ramcke and would prepare to attack eastwards along the coastal road and plain, as the enemy's defences were threatened by the movement round the south flank of the third battle group, Obserst Utz's three mountain battalions. Utz was to start at once.

Gericke and his mixed force of survivors from the 4th and 1st Battalions of the Storm Regiment, reinforced by the parachute companies dropped the day before, had already followed up the New Zealanders withdrawing from their counter-attack, and now held Pirgos firmly. Further movement forward met stiff resistance, but under Ramcke's new orders they all prepared to attack again on the next day, 23 May.

Early next morning Gericke, watching from Pirgos village, saw clear signs of the New Zealand battalions withdrawing and very soon afterwards, the Ramcke Battle Group began their advance.

For the next eight days heavy fighting continued, until on 1 June those British Forces, who had not been taken off by the Royal Navy, surrendered and Crete was in German hands.

It had been a costly operation. In the twelve days of the battle the Germans had lost 3,968 men killed in Crete and a further 327 drowned at sea. 1,738 German soldiers and airmen had been wounded and 17 taken prisoner. 147 aircraft had been damaged by enemy fire or rough landings. Most of the aircraft lost were Ju52 transports, but against these losses should be set the facts that the Ju52s brought into Crete 23,464 men, 539 guns and mortars and 1,000 tonnes of supplies.

The German Air Force and their Airborne Forces had certainly won a major victory, fighting with skill, courage and persistence. They had killed 1,742 men of the British and New Zealand forces and wounded another 1,737. They had captured 11,835 prisoners of war and in the damaging attacks by the Luftwaffe on the ships of the Royal Navy, no less than 2,011 men were drowned or killed in action. It was a major disaster for the Allies.

On 20 July 1941 General Student reported in person to Adolf Hitler and was shocked to hear

Below: General Student, the founder of German Airborne Forces, is shown round by one of his parachute battalion commanders. Note the latter's binoculars and map-case. He is still wearing his jump overall, as is his orderly behind him with the holstered Luger.

him say 'the days of parachute troops are over. The parachute weapon depends on surprise and that has now gone'.

Hitler and the General Staff had been appalled by the losses in Crete, where the Germans had lost by the end of the first day's fighting more men than in the whole war so far. They were never again to use airborne assault as a method of strategic or tactical attack, although they were to exploit to the full the psychological value of parachute training by raising a parachute army of 100,000 men to fight as ground troops for the rest of the war.

Student himself went on to command the First Parachute Army in Holland and survived the war. He now lives quietly in southern Germany. Eugen Meindl recovered from his chest wound and played a large part in raising the new parachute divisions. He commanded a division in Russia during the winter of 1941/42 and then led the II Parachute Corps through battles in Italy, Normandy, Holland and Germany. His corps played a major part in the bitter defence of the Rhineland in February and March 1945 and he continued to hold the affection and respect of his old soldiers until his death in 1951.

General Student's chief of staff, General Schlemm, took over the First Parachute Army east of the Rhine in March 1945, until he was badly wounded in an air attack on his headquarters on 21 March. Gericke raised a new

2nd Parachute Regiment from the survivors of his 4th Battalion and the 1st Battalion were expanded to form a new Storm Regiment to fight in Tunisia under Koch, but he was killed in 1942 in a car accident on an autobahn in Germany. Stenzler's 2nd Battalion went to Russia, as did most of the XI Flieger Korps, and were totally destroyed in the battle for Leningrad, Stenzler himself being killed there in February 1942. The 3rd Battalion was never reformed after its shattering losses at Maleme.

Oberst Bernhard Hermann Ramcke led the newly raised 2nd Parachute Division in Russia from November 1943 to March 1944 and in June 1944 joined Meindle's parachute corps in Brittany. From 12 August to 20 September he and his Division held Brest against the American attacks under General Middleton in a siege which won for him the Knight's Cross with Oakleaves, Swords and Diamonds.

Crete was both a triumph for German Airborne Troops and the death of their hopes for assault from the air. As General Kurt Student, the 'father of airborne forces', heard Hitler's fatal words, so in that same month General Bill Lee in America and General Boy Browning in Great Britain received from their Governments the word to press on with all speed, to form the massive airborne forces which were to fight in North Africa, Sicily, Normandy, Holland and over the Rhine.

Below: A familiar sight in Crete — the graves of German parachute soldiers. After the war most German cemeteries were ploughed up by the Cretans, but a large number of their men lie buried in the German cemetery on top of Hill 107 at Maleme.

CORREGIDOR

A stick of seven men, watched by
men from the previous aircraft,
who have just missed the pre-war
officers' swimming pool near the
parade ground.

Corregidor~1945

By mid-February 1945 General MacArthur's United States forces were well on the way to smashing the Japanese 14th Area Army in Luzon, the largest island of the Philippines. Corregidor, the rocky, fortress island in the entrance to Manila Bay, was never a key feature in General Yamashita's defence plans, since he intended to withdraw his main forces into mountain strongholds, as the Americans advanced from their main amphibious landings in the Lingayen Gulf.

Yet as long as Corregidor was held by the Japanese, its guns could deny the use of Manila Bay to Allied shipping. Even more important to General MacArthur and to most Americans was the urge to recapture Corregidor, the scene of the Americans' last stand against the Japanese in May 1942. It was from Corregidor that MacArthur himself left the Philippines, embarking at night in a motor torpedo boat and slipping through the encircling Japanese fleet.

Accordingly General Headquarters South West Pacific Area gave orders on 3 February to General Krueger's Sixth Army for the capture of Corregidor. General Krueger planned a combined airborne and amphibious assault and set 16 February as D-Day.

The troops allotted to the attack were the 503rd Parachute Infantry and their supporting artillery from the 11th Airborne Division for the airborne assault and the 3rd Battalion 34th Infantry from the 24th Division for the landing from the sea.

Corregidor lies in the narrow entrance to Manila Bay, two miles from the Bataan shore to the north and eight miles from the mainland to the south. Between Corregidor and this south shore were two other islands, Caballo and the reef of El Fraile, on which US Army Engineers had built the concrete Fort Drum in the shape of a battleship with four 14-inch guns and four 6-inch guns. These had been destroyed in the 1942

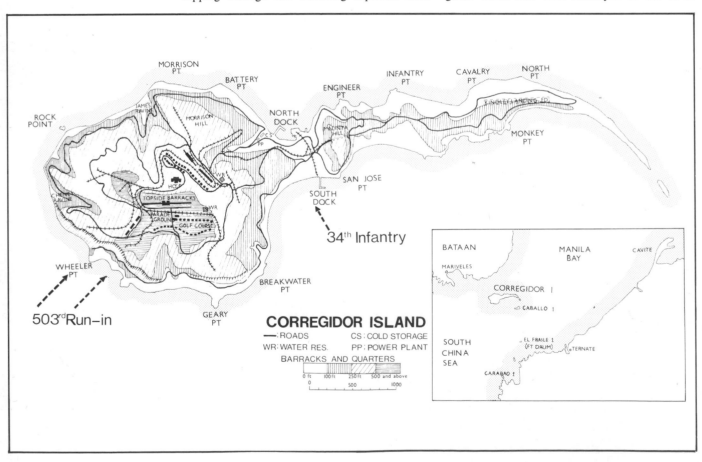

CORREGIDOR ISLAND
—: ROADS   CS: COLD STORAGE
WR: WATER RES.   PP: POWER PLANT
BARRACKS AND QUARTERS

fighting and never replaced by the Japanese. Corregidor, however, was still a formidable fortress. Shaped like a tadpole, its round head at the western end rose to a small plateau 500 feet above the sea, with steep cliffs on the north, west and south. This was 'Topside' to two generations of American soldiers before World War II and on it were the main barracks and parade ground, the officers' married quarters and a small golf course. To the east the ground sloped down gradually over 'Middleside' to a narrow waist, only 600 yards wide with sandy beaches to north and south. This was 'Bottomside' and there was a North and a South Dock, from which roads and a light railway led to the various barracks, stores and batteries on the island.

Immediately east of Bottomside rose Malinta Hill, some 350 feet high and extensively tunnelled for the main road and for stores and magazines. Beyond Malinta the island narrowed to form the tadpole's tail of sandy, wooded land, nowhere more than 150 feet above the waters of the bay. At the eastern end of Corregidor was Kindley Field, a disused and overgrown landing strip. Topside had been built up by the Americans into a modern fortress. Its gun batteries not only commanded the sea approaches to Manila Bay but could also sweep the Corregidor beaches. It was well provided with underground stores, magazines and communicating tunnels. When the Japanese assault troops landed on the northern beaches of Bottomside in 1942, they had lost half their men under fire from Topside. The plan of attack, based on Sixth Army Intelligence that now in 1945 the Japanese garrison was only 850 men, included dropping 2,000 parachutists and landing 1,000 men from the sea on 16 February, followed by another 1,000 parachute troops on the next day. Colonel M. Jones, commanding the 503rd Parachute Infantry, stationed at Mindoro, flew over Corregidor to look for drop zones and chose Kindley Field at the east end. It seemed the only possible place. General Krueger at once overruled this on the grounds that this DZ would be too far from the main objective Topside; that surprise would be lost; and that both the DZ and the approach to the western end of the island would be swept by Japanese fire.

There were only two other places, the parade ground in front of the main barracks on Topside only 325 yards long and 250 yards wide, and the sloping golf course just south east of the officers' houses, which was 350 yards by 185 yards. The rest of Topside was a mass of broken ground, ruined buildings and splintered trees, while even the parade ground and golf course were covered in bomb craters, debris and tangled undergrowth grown up since 1942. The ground fell away sharply from the golf course to a steep cliff. There was no margin for error at either place.

The forecast wind was easterly at 15 to 20mph with gusts to a higher speed. Each jumper would take about half a second to leave the plane and at the dropping speed for a C-47 of 110mph, the maximum permissible time over each DZ would be six seconds, if the men were not to go over the cliffs. If they jumped at 400 feet above ground, their time of descent would be 25 seconds and in the forecast wind their drift might be 250 feet westwards. On these figures the 503rd and the 317th Troop Carrier Group planned to fly in to each DZ in line astern from south west to north east. West to east would have been better from the dropping angle, but would bring the two columns of aircraft too close together. Each C-47 would drop six or seven men at a time and then circle back for another two passes. They calculated it would take an hour to drop a thousand men.

The planes were then to return to Mindoro for a second lift, which should reach the ground five hours after the first. It was a bold plan, contravening the most important principle of airborne assault, concentration in time and space, and Colonel Jones himself thought that half his men might be injured in the drop. Surprise was going to be all-important. The seaborne attack by the 3rd Battalion 34th Infantry was timed to land two hours after the first drop and it was hoped this might distract the Japanese defence. The 34th would then seize the key feature of Malinta Hill and provide a secure means of evacuating the wounded and supplying the whole attacking force, before the defenders could recover from the preliminary air and sea bombardment. For the accurate bombing and shelling of the Japanese defences and for the pin-point dropping of the 503rd, daylight was essential and so they fixed 8.30am for the parachute drop and 10.30am for the boats to hit the beach.

Captain Akira Itagaki of the Imperial Japanese Navy commanded the garrison of Corregidor. They numbered 5,000 men and not 850 as forecast by American Intelligence. They were mostly sailors, organised into provisional units and assigned to the various defence sectors, but there were also three infantry companies and two artillery batteries from the army. Itagaki's strongest positions, manned by half his force, covered the main access routes to Topside at the James, Cheney and Ramsey Ravines and held Malinta Hill. The remainder of the men were held in reserve at Malinta Hill and in the tunnels below, with a few men in beach defence positions along the tail of the island. The headquarters were underground at Topside with telephone links to each defensive position and battery. There were no lateral communications between each position and if the telephone exchange on Topside were to be knocked out, control would be lost.

On 22 January the United States Army Air Forces began to pound Corregidor. Between this date and 16 February, the day of the assault, the Fifth and Thirteenth Air Forces dropped 3,125 tons of bombs, mostly on Topside, Bottomside and Malinta. Early in the morning of 16 February 24 Liberator heavy bombers attacked all known and suspected gun positions and 11 Mitchell

Above: 503rd Parachute Infantry in a
C-47 on their way to Corregidor
— Private Yocum, First Sergeant
Baldwin, Privates Macdonald,
Boone, Yekinak, Narrow, Pearson
and McCurry. They are wearing
life jackets and carrying
grenades./*All photographs in this
chapter US Army*

Right: The same stick standing to
the door. Sergeant Baldwin is still
puffing at his cigar.

medium bombers struck at anti-aircraft guns and defence positions on the south shore. Thirty-one fighter bombers shot up and bombed any targets they could see, both on Corregidor and the island of Caballo, a mile to the south.

On 13 February, three days before the assault, the United States Navy joined in. Five light cruisers and nine destroyers of Admiral Berkey's Task Force 77 opened fire, mostly engaging the guns on the north face of Topside and Malinta. Next day the Japanese return fire succeeded in damaging two destroyers and hit a minesweeper so severely that she had to be sunk. By the end of the day the Japanese guns were still firing and the US ships were running short of shells. On 15 February three heavy cruisers and five more destroyers arrived from Admiral Kinkaid's fleet in the Lingayen Gulf and joined in the bombardment. By now every building above ground on Corregidor was in ruins, every tree was a splintered stump and the ground was covered in bomb craters, shell holes and debris. Many of the Japanese guns had been knocked out, but some were still in action and most of the garrison had survived in the shelter of the tunnels and caves.

At dawn on 16 February the men of the 3rd Battalion, 503rd Parachute Infantry, of Battery C 462nd Parachute Field Artillery, Company C 161st Airborne Engineers and most of the 503rd's regimental headquarters, climbed into the C-47s of the 317th Troop Carrier Group on Mindoro and took off for Corregidor. At the same time the 3rd Battalion 34th Infantry prepared to embark in 25 landing craft of the 529th Engineer Boat and Shore Regiment on the southern tip of Bataan. Ships of the US Navy moved in towards the south shore of Bottomside, ready to blast the defences as the amphibious craft closed the beach. Motor torpedo boats stood by, just out of gun range, with orders to dash in to the rescue of any men who dropped over the cliffs or into the sea.

It was a fine, clear day, but the wind was stronger than expected, over 20mph, and blowing from the north-west.

As the two lines of C-47s came in sight to the south west, 70 fighter-bombers dived on to Malinta Hill, the eastern end of Corregidor and Caballo. Above the two columns of aircraft circled a single C-47, from which Colonel Jones and the group commander of the 317th watched the drop and prepared to radio corrections as necessary to the incoming planes. By now the flotilla of landing craft had left Marivelos and were setting course to round the western end of Corregidor, escorted by three destroyers with minesweepers ahead of them.

The leading C-47s in each column were over the parade ground and the golf course almost together at 8.32am and switched on their green

Below: The first lift dropping on the parade ground in the left centre and on the golf course at the bottom right corner. Topside barracks, battered in 1942 and 1945, stand out clearly. The mountains behind are on Bataan.

Above: The moment of touch-down — feet and knees together, eyes on the ground, hands on the lift-webs, ready to pull down the second before impact.

jump light just beyond the drop zones, allowing for the westerly drift. The first man hit the ground at 8.33 and although some of the sticks were on target, most of the men landed off the drop zones among the ruined buildings and trees and a few were over the cliff below the golf course. The two Colonels overhead realised at once that the aircraft were dropping too high, at 550 feet instead of 400, and ordered a progressive reduction in altitude to the following aircraft. No one fired at the leading aircraft, but those following met sporadic machine gun and rifle fire. A few, small groups of Japanese on the drop zones were killed or driven off. By 9.45am the first lift was completed and about 250 men, a quarter of those dropped, had been injured, some seriously and some lightly. Colonel Jones's command aircraft ran in last and he jumped out to join the men on the ground. Lying off Geary Point was PT Boat 376, commanded by Lieutenant John Mapp, and seeing several parachutes come down on the cliff and on the

narrow beach below the golf course, he ran his boat in to 30 yards from the shore, lowered a rubber dinghy and brought off seven men of the 503rd under rifle and machine gun fire from caves in the cliff. A little later they rescued ten more men in the same way.

Most of the men dropped over the cliffs survived and some of them made a significant contribution to the outcome of the battle. Japanese look-outs on Topside warned Captain Itagaki at about 8.30, that they could see landing craft leaving Marivelos and setting course for the western end of Corregidor. He had been told to expect an airborne attack, but considered a parachute landing out of the question. The air above him had been alive with American bombers and fighters since first light and both he and his look-outs probably mistook the approaching C-47s for another wave of medium bombers. With a small escort he hurried down to an observation post near Breakwater Point, presumably to watch for the approaching invasion from the sea. As he got there, 25 to 30 American parachute soldiers landed all round him. The Japanese opened fire on them, but the Americans got out of their clumsy, five buckle, parachute harness in record time, assembled as a squad and attacked the OP. Captain Itagaki and the eight men with him were killed. The central communications centre on Topside had already been destroyed and now effective command of the Japanese garrison ceased. Each group of Japanese sailors and soldiers were on their own, but true to the Japanese tradition, all but 20 of them fought to the death during the next two weeks.

By 10am the drop zones were secure and the 3rd Battalion 503rd were beginning the slow and dangerous business of clearing the Japanese out of every battery, building, tunnel and trench. Two .50 calibre machine guns were set up above Ramsey Ravine so that they could give covering fire on to the southern beach of Bottomside for the amphibious landing, due in half an hour, and although their fire was not needed in the event, the gun crews had a grandstand view of the landing.

As the landing craft neared the shore, two LC1(R)s launched their salvos of multiple rockets, drenching the beach with a devastating shower of explosions and simultaneously one of them, LC1 338, was hit four times by Japanese 3-inch shells. The leading boats touched down at 10.28am, two minutes early, and the first four waves of infantry ran ashore without a shot being fired. Only as the fifth wave landed did the Japanese defences come to life and machine guns opened fire from Ramsey Ravine, Breakwater Point and San Jose Point. On the beach itself a Sherman tank and an M7 gun on its tracked carrier blew up on mines and a 37mm anti-tank gun being towed by a jeep was also destroyed. Thirty minutes from touch-down Companies K and L of the 34th Infantry had reached the top of

Top: Private Goen's photo of men landing on the golf course.

Above: Men landing on the golf course. Caballo Island in the background.

Left: Another view of the golf course.

67

Above: The parade ground and golf course drop zones on Topside. The barracks, the hospital behind and the line of officers' quarters are visible. In the foreground are the cliffs with six parachutes scattered down them. The C-47 is flying over the North Dock on Bottomside and towards the north of Malinta Hill.

Left: A closer look at the parade ground drop zone, the barracks and hospital at the left edge, the two rows of quarters with the water tanks and lighthouse between them and beyond is Bottomside with its North and South Docks and beaches. Malinta Hill is shrouded in smoke from bursting naval shells.

Above right: LCMs and LCIs carrying the 3rd Bn 34th Infantry to the San Jose beach.

Centre right: LCI's beached at San Jose. Three LCM's are this side of them. A tank is moving inland from the centre LCM past the ambulance and a bulldozer is working in the foreground.

Bottom right: LST's pulling back from the beach after landing Alligators — lightly armoured, tracked amphibians — from the 3rd Battalion, 34th Infantry.

Malinta Hill and only two men had been killed and six wounded. It had been easier than anyone had expected and can only be explained by the probability that the Japanese had been driven below ground by the air and naval bombardment, which had gone on right up to the time of the drop, and had become confused by the combined parachute and sea-borne attack.

Up on Topside some of the officers in the 3rd Battalion 503rd were pleasantly surprised by the lack of serious Japanese opposition, but considerably concerned by the number of jump injuries caused by the high wind speed and the small, rough drop zones. It was suggested that the second lift be cancelled, but Colonel Jones decided to let it come.

At 12.40pm the 2nd Battalion 503rd began dropping together with the rest of Battery B, 462nd Parachute Artillery, the 503rd's Service Company and the rest of their headquarters. It was a good drop with fewer casualties than in the first lift, in spite of being fired on by a Japanese 20mm gun and two American .50 calibre machine guns, which had been dropped wide and brought into action by the enemy. Altogether some 2,050 men had jumped that morning, of whom 20 were killed and 50 wounded by Japanese fire and 210 were injured in landing. This casualty rate of 14% was well below the gloomy forecasts of 20% or even 50%, and was rapidly reduced, as the less seriously injured men soon returned to active duty.

During the afternoon Colonel Jones cancelled the drop for next day, 17 February, and asked for his 1st Battalion to be brought in by sea. He ordered the 2nd Battalion to take over the security of the drop zones and the 3rd Battalion to continue cleaning out Topside. Company H cleared the barracks and the hospital behind them and went on to dig in round a knoll to the north east, which looked over the whole of Topside. Company G advanced down the slope to Middleside and made contact with the sea-borne battalion that evening. Fifty five more men were wounded before nightfall and there were still plenty of Japanese, full of fight, in the caves and tunnels on the west and south of the drop zones.

Next day the 1st Battalion 503rd landed from the sea at Bottomside and moved up to join the rest of the regiment. For the next seven days the three parachute battalions methodically cleared the whole of Topside and the west of the island. Each Japanese position was first attacked from the air with napalm or liquid fire or bombarded from the sea, if its location permitted. As the last shell or bomb landed, the infantry attacked, covered by direct, close range fire from 75mm howitzers and 37mm anti-tank guns. The riflemen and sub-machine gunners covered the assault teams, who moved in under cover of phosphorous smoke grenades with flame throwers. A wet shot into the casemate or cave-mouth or down a tunnel or a ventilation shaft was followed by a flame shot and gouts of flame and smoke shot out

Above left: The second lift of the 2nd Battalion, 503rd Parachute Infantry, dropping on to the golf course.

Left: The guns arrive — C-47's dropping 75mm pack howitzers.

Above: Another stick of seven men, seen from the old lighthouse and water-tank.

Right: The ruined barracks on Topsides and parachutes on the parade ground. The 503rd's command post was set up in the centre part of the barracks.

Right: Comfortable duty for one of the 503rd, watching Malinta Hill from a water-tower on Topside.

Below: A squad, ready to cover with their rifles and sub-machine guns, the final assault with flame throwers and explosives on a cave entrance.

Far right, top: Men of the 3rd Battalion, 503rd, moving towards Breakwater Point. The effects of the naval and air bombardment are obvious. Above the destroyer is Caballo Island.

Far right, bottom: Photo taken by Private Morris Weiner of a soldier of the 503rd aiming his bazooka at a Japanese strongpoint on Topside. He is carrying an M1 carbine, two water-bottles and his steel helmet. Above him is a parachute, discarded in the initial drop.

of each opening. If the Japanese were still alive, the engineers blew in the cave and tunnel entrances and finally entombed them.

Each night small groups of Japanese sailors and soldiers tried to recapture positions already cleared and this they were welcome to do, where the position made an easy killing ground. To prevent enemy movement the underground passages and tunnels were systematically blown in. On the second day, 17 February, over 300 Japanese were killed and a further 775 on the 18th. In these same two days, Rock Force, the 503rd and the 3rd/34th, lost 30 men killed and 110 wounded. It was a slow, dangerous and bloody business.

On the third day, 19 February, at 2 o'clock in the morning 40 Japanese blew up an underground ammunition dump, a few hundred yards inland from Breakwater Point, killing themselves and killing and wounding 20 men of the 503rd in a building above them. That same morning 400 Japanese, from their positions at Cheney Ravine and Wheeler Point, attacked up towards Topside and some of them penetrated as far as the barracks. Pte Lloyd McCarter won the Medal of Honour in this action and the 503rd succeeded in first holding the attack and then killing all 400, except for three men taken prisoner, the first of the whole operation. American losses this day were 30 killed and 75 wounded.

Lloyd McCarter had already distinguished himself on the first day, soon after the drop, by rushing a Japanese machine gun post over 30 yards of open ground under heavy fire and killing the crew with grenades. Two days later he killed six more Japanese riflemen, firing from caves and bunkers and now, in this major Japanese counter-attack, he held out alone when all the men with him had been wounded. When his sub-machine gun ran out of ammunition, he continued to fight with a Browning Automatic rifle and then with an M1 rifle. In the Japanese final assault soon after first light on 19 February he stood up, the better to see and engage the enemy, and even after he was wounded he insisted on pointing out where the enemy were. He had killed more than 30 Japanese.

So the fighting went grinding on for four more days, until on 23 February the Japanese suvivors on Topside made a last, desperate banzai charge and were shot dead.

Colonel Jones now turned his attention to the eastern half of Corregidor. The 3rd Battalion 34th Infantry had been busy enough in the last seven days clearing out Japanese from Middleside and Bottomside and holding the top surface of Malinta Hill. The Japanese had made several attacks on them from the tunnels inside Malinta and from the east end of the island and the 34th had lost ten men killed and as many wounded. Everyone's main concern was the probability of some desperate act by the 2,000 Japanese in the Malinta Hill tunnels, where there were known to be tons of ammunition and explosives.

Above: Pte Lloyd McCarter.

Right: 'Jungle Express' — a C-47 dropping supplies on 17 February. Below are the old officers' quarters and beyond is the golf course.

At 9.30pm on 21 February these expectations were fulfilled. A colossal explosion shook the whole of Malinta Hill. Fissures appeared on its surface, rocks and debris flew into the air and flames shot out of every tunnel entrance, gun port and ventilation shaft. Six men of the 34th were buried alive by a landslide and, although a few hundred Japanese escaped to the east in the confusion and the dust-filled darkness, most of the 2,000 Japanese in the tunnels were killed by the explosion. Two nights later several more heavy explosions inside the hill marked where the last of the Japanese there had committed suicide.

On 24 February the 1st and 3rd Battalions of the 503rd advanced eastwards, leaving their 2nd Battalion and the 34th Infantry to hold Malinta Hill and Topside. Supported by air and naval bombardment and their own guns, the parachute infantry slowly worked down the tail of Corregidor, crushing resistance at Engineer and Infantry Points and killing 300 out of 600 Japanese who tried to counter-attack. By night-fall they were only 3,000 yards from the eastern end of the island. That same day the 3rd Battalion of the 34th left Corregidor to rejoin their division and to prepare for further operations in the southern Philippines. They were replaced by the 1st Battalion, 151st Infantry. Next day the 503rd moved on, until only 1,000 yards from the eastern end of the island. Banzai charges near Monkey Point cost more Japanese lives and many of the survivors took to the water in an attempt to swim to Bataan or Caballo. Two hundred of them, who would not surrender, were killed in the water by the circling PT boats and landing craft and it is believed another 800 must have drowned.

A few minutes after 11am on 26 February another and even bigger series of explosions shook the whole eastern end of the island, as the Japanese blew up the underground magazine at Monkey Point. A mile away on Topside a man was injured by a flying rock. Debris fell on the deck of a destroyer 2,000 yards offshore. A Sherman tank was thrown through the air for 50 yards and it took an oxy-acetylene cutter, borrowed from a destroyer by the 503rd, to release the sole survivor of the crew. The ground was spattered with the human fragments of 200 Japanese sailors and soldiers and 50 Americans and when the dust settled, there was a broad, shallow depression, where before had stood a small hill. It took an hour and a half to clear the many wounded and the US Army official history quotes a doctor there as saying 'As soon as I got all the casualties off, I sat down on a rock and burst out crying. I couldn't stop myself and didn't want to. I had seen more than a man could stand and still stay normal... when I had the cases to care for, that kept me going; but after that it was too much'.

At 4pm men of the 503rd reached the eastern tip of the island, but only four days later could Colonel Jones say with certainty that Corregidor was clear of Japanese. Even then he was not strictly accurate for, in 1946, a year after the final Japanese surrender, 20 men came out of the Corregidor caves to give themselves up.

Below: Another shot of the same aircraft on the same run. Part of the battery below the golf course can be seen to the right of the picture.

Right: General Douglas MacArthur landing at South Dock from a US Navy PT (or motor torpedo) boat on 2 March. It was on just such a PT boat that he left Corregidor in May 1942. Colonel Jones of the 503rd greets him with a salute and on this side is an infantry officer, probably the commanding officer of the 151st Infantry, who has clearly had his drill uniform washed and ironed.

Below: General MacArthur is driven off from South Dock to Topside . . .

Right: . . . and through the heavily bombed and shelled surface of Bottomside.

Below: The US Flag is hoisted on the original pole. The guard of honour is from the 503rd, in front of whom is Colonel Jones. General MacArthur, in light coloured drill uniform and a peaked cap, is the tall figure with his back to the camera in front of the group in the foreground.

Bottom: Photo taken in 1961 by Specialist Steve Moore from almost the same spot. The two dead trees are still there and the ruined barracks, but the ground is once more disappearing into jungle.

The United States Army had lost 215 men killed and 450 more wounded. Another 240 had been injured. Out of these 1,005 casualties, 780 were men of the 503rd Parachute Infantry and their parachute gunners. They counted no less than 4,500 Japanese bodies and believed that there were 500 more sealed in the underground tunnels and magazines. Only 20 Japanese were taken prisoner. It had been a costly affair, and a rough and unorthodox parachute operation. Yet they were glad they had done it. Today, 32 years later, men are proud to remember that they were with the 503rd on Corregidor.

On 2 March General Douglas MacArthur landed at South Dock from a PT boat, returning in the same way as he had left in 1942. He was driven up to the Topside Parade Ground, where parachutes still hung in the trees and a guard of honour from the 503rd were drawn up opposite the flagstaff. Most of Rock Force were watching as he got out of his jeep, carrying a United States Flag, and Colonel Jones met him with a salute and the words:

'Sir, I present to you Fortress Corregidor'.

MacArthur gave the flag to the NCO by the flagstaff and said:

'I see the old flagstaff still stands. Hoist the Colours to its peak and let no enemy ever haul them down again.'

Then he and all the spectators saluted, as Old Glory went up and the guard presented arms. Colonel Jones then took his Commander-in-Chief on a tour of the island and MacArthur spoke to many of the men. At Malinta tunnel he listened to the story of the explosion and the slaughter there and said: 'It was bad enough for us when we were here, but it was worse for them. They have set the pattern for their own annihilation'.

Then he turned, kicked a shell-case out of his path and walked away.

77

THE RHINE

438th Troop Carrier Group
dropping the 507th near Diersfordt.
The C-47 'Goonie Birds' are
turning away to the south and west.
The dim mass of the Diersfordter
forest can be seen below. Both this
picture and that on the title page,
were taken by Sergeant Fred
Quandt from a B-17 Flying
Fortress, which was shot down a
few minutes later./US Army

Operation Varsity

By mid-January 1945 the Battle of the Ardennes was over and Adolf Hitler's last attempt to wrest the initiative from the Allies had failed. Both sides had suffered heavy losses in men, tanks and guns, but whereas the Allies could replace them in a few weeks, the German Army had used its last reserves.

By early March the British and Americans had fought their way forward to the Rhine against bitter resistance. In 21 Army Group in the north Field Marshal Montgomery's aim now was to cross the Rhine between Wesel and Emmerich in massive strength and to secure a bridgehead on the east bank, from which his armoured and infantry divisions could burst out into the north German plain. Both General Simpson's Ninth US and General Dempsey's Second British Armies were to cross at the same time and the latter was to have the XVIII Airborne Corps under command for the crossing. General Dempsey decided to attack with two corps forward, each with one division assaulting over the Rhine during the night of 23/24 March and others following up. The two divisions of the Airborne Corps, the US 17th and the British 6th, were to land by day east of the river, after the main crossings had begun, and within range of the artillery massed on the west bank.

Opposite Xanten, where the 15th Scottish Division was to cross, the country consisted of flat water-meadows, separated by drainage ditches and criss-crossed with unmetalled roads and tracks, connecting small villages and farms. Two miles to the east the wooded ridge of the Diersfordter Wald ran parallel to the Rhine and dominated the low-lying land along the river. A mile beyond these woods the river Issel, 40 metres wide, ran between steep banks and beyond that again a half-completed and abandoned autobahn.

Since August 1944 the British and American airborne divisions and troop carrier air forces had been grouped together in the First Allied Airborne Army, commanded by an American Army Air Force officer, Lieutenant General Lewis H. Brereton, who had planned an imaginative parachute operation as far back as 1918. For the Rhine crossing he had established his headquarters at Maison Lafitte, near Paris, with a command post at Second Tactical Air Force in Brussels beside Air Marshal Sir Arthur Coningham, who was to command all air operations. The immediate control of all aircraft in the battle area was given to the RAF's 83 Group, so that there was no doubt as to who was in command and no delay in the decision to switch as necessary the massive air power available. One of the lessons of Arnhem had been learned. Both the British 6th and the American 17th Airborne Divisons were to land on top of their objectives, the German rear defences and gun areas in the Diersfordter Forest, benefiting from another Arnhem lesson and avoiding the drawback, so fatal for the British 1st Airborne Division, of a long approach march. A third lesson from Arnhem, the perils of a slow build-up over several days, led now to the decision to drop both divisions simultaneously in one lift.

Below: Illingworth Cartoon — 'The N th Army' — a graphic illustration, published in *Punch* after Arnhem, of the 'threat in being' posed to Germany by the First Allied Airborne Army./*Published by permission of the Editor of Punch*

Above: American technicians
assemble a Waco CG4A
glider./*USAF*

Left: Eleven Apaches of the 17th
Division — fancy hair-cuts seem to
be a standard transit camp
phenomenon./*IWM*

193rd Glider Infantry were disbanded and the men sent to make the 194th up to three battalions. Each glider artillery battalion increased from two to three batteries and one of them had to convert from the airborne 75mm pack howitzer to the normal field gun, the 105mm. Each of the parachute rifle platoons took on a third squad and a new parachute field artillery battalion, the 464th, arrived from the States.

In the six weeks before the operation commanders and staffs were also involved in detailed planning and briefing, in moving their units out to twelve marshalling areas near their take-off airfields and in despatching two thousand jeeps and trucks to the west bank of the Rhine, ready to join up, once bridges had been built.

All this hustle was well within the scope of their commanding General, William M. Miley, who had raised and commanded the US First Parachute Battalion in September 1940. Another experienced parachutist was Colonel Edson D. Raff, commanding the 507th Parachute Infantry. He had been the commanding officer of the 2nd Battalion, 503rd Parachute Infantry, who had in July 1942 joined the British 1st Airborne

These two divisions formed the XVIII Airborne Corps, commanded by Major General Matthew B. Ridgway, who had led the US 82nd Airborne Division into Normandy. Major General Richard Gale, his deputy, had commanded the 6th from its formation in 1943. Both men were able and experienced leaders, who liked and respected each other, and the whole Anglo/American Corps worked smoothly and cheerfully together. The British 6th Division on Salisbury Plain in England had moved back in January from a month in the Ardennes and in Holland. They were at full strength, well rested and in a high state of training. Their general was now Eric Bols and there was a new commander of the 6th Airlanding Brigade, Hugh Bellamy. The 3rd and 5th Parachute Brigades were still led by James Hill and Nigel Poett, who had taken them to Normandy. Of the nine commanding officers of battalions, eight had fought with the Division since D-Day. The ninth was Jeff Nicklin, a large, robust and determined figure, who had played top-class Canadian football and who demanded from the 1st Canadian Parachute Battalion strict standards of discipline and efficiency. The US 17th were still in the Ardennes on the River Our in contact with the German V Panzer Army, who were retreating from the failure of the Ardennes offensive, and the 17th only moved back to Chalons in France on 10 February. Their camps were not completed; the spring thaw had made them into mud-baths; there were no proper roads or latrines; and it took four days of hard work by every man in the division to make the camps habitable. They were 4,000 men under strength, and not only had the reinforcements to be trained but the division was to re-organise on a new establishment. The

Far left, top: Major General Matthew B. Ridgway, commanding XVIII Airborne Corps, and Major General Eric Bols, GOC 6th Airborne Division, taken in Wismar on VE Day.

Far left, bottom: Lieutenant Colonel Jeff Nicklin, commanding 1st Canadian Parachute Battalion, killed in the trees on the DZ.

Left: Eric Bols driving Brigadier James Hill, commander of 3rd Parachute Brigade, some days after the Rhine crossing. In the back are the ADC and a military police bodyguard. Reserve petrol cans are strapped to the front bumper, a major general's two star plate is screwed to the radiator and the jeep is flying the general's command pennant — red with a blue Pegasus.

Below: Two men of the 194th Glider Infantry pose for the press on an airfield in France./USAF

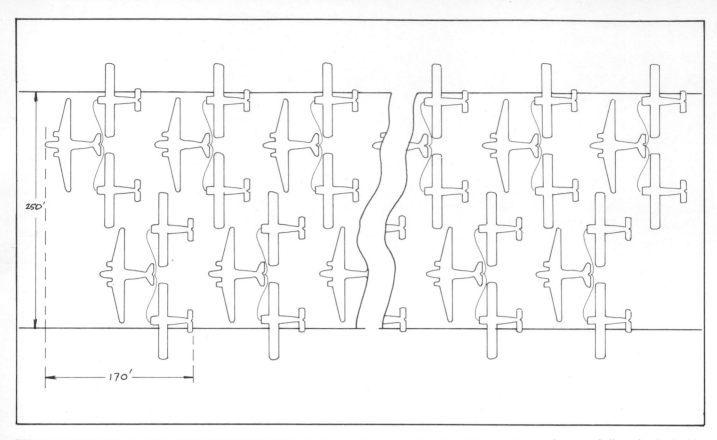

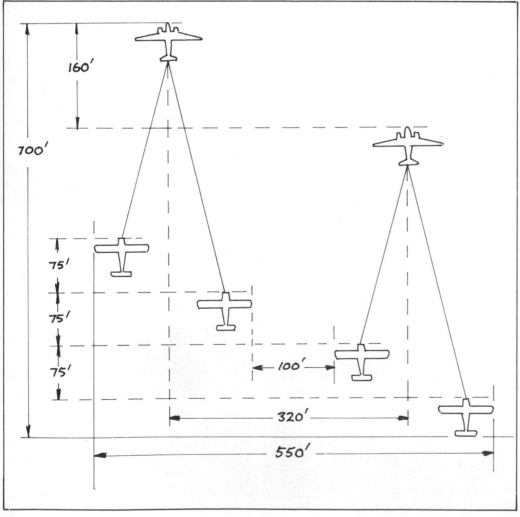

Above: Marshalling plan for double-tow gliders and C-47 tugs — part of the IX Troop Carrier Command orders.

Left and above right: Single and double tow formation diagram from the same orders.

Right: WACO gliders of the 439th Troop Carrier Group, lined up at Chateaudun, ready for loading and emplaning by the 194th Glider Infantry on 23 March./*USAF*

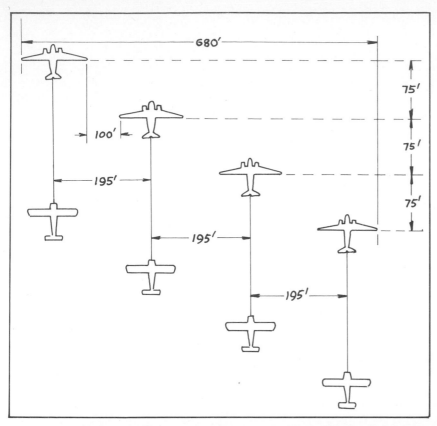

Division and had made the first American operational jump outside Oran in November of that year. In Normandy the 507th had formed part of the 82nd Airborne Division and had suffered severely from a scattered drop, but they still had a nucleus of experienced leaders. The rest of the 17th Division had only been in action in the later stages of the Battle of the Ardennes.

The American groups in IX Troop Carrier Command had to prepare 12 battered and neglected airfields. Only 34 days were available to improve run-ways and to build taxi-tracks, marshalling areas, dispersal areas and access roads, to fill in bomb craters, repair drainage and lay glider parks and to provide accommodation for stores, officers and men. Three thousand United States, British and Canadian army engineers and 750 French civilians worked a 24-hour schedule and, urged on by Colonel Burbridge, the Command engineer officer, they laid thousands of tons of steel planking, hardcore, tar and bitumen.

The defence of the Rhine in the north, opposite Second Army, was in the hands of the German First Parachute Army, whose commander, General Schlemm, had been General Student's chief of staff for the battle of Crete in 1941. He had fought in Russia and Italy and in November

Right: Loading a medical jeep into a Waco glider./*IWM*

Below: Major General Bud Miley, commanding the 17th Airborne Division, has a few last words with Brigadier General Floyd Parks, Chief of Staff First Allied Airborne Army, before emplaning./*US Army*

Far right, top: Some of the 507th march to their aircraft in the early morning of 24 March./*IWM*

Far right, centre: Men of the 194th Glider Infantry wait to emplane in the early morning of the same day./*IWM*

Far right, bottom: C-47 tugs and Waco gliders lined up with tow-ropes attached, ready for take-off./*IWM*

1944 had taken over command of the First Parachute Army. He led them through the bitter fighting for the Reichswald and had contrived the orderly withdrawal of the II Parachute Corps from the final bridgehead in front of Wesel — encouraged by Hitler's message, that if he lost a Rhine bridge intact he would be shot. The northernmost of his three corps now was this same II Parachute Corps, led by General Meindl, who had commanded the Storm Regiment at Maleme in Crete. His corps included the 6th, 7th and 8th Parachute Divisions, who had borne the brunt of the battle for the Reichswald. Each division was down to 3 or 4,000 men with few heavy weapons and a shortage of ammunition, but they were still effective fighting units, supported by nearly 200 guns.

To the south of the Parachute Corps the Rhine was held by the LXXXVI Infantry Corps, commanded by General Straube, whose 84th Infantry Division linked up with the 7th Parachute Division at the north end of the Diersfordter Wald. They too had lost heavily in the Reichwald fighting and many of their reinforcements were men of low medical category. Eight battalions of Volkssturm, made up of older men called up for home defence, reached the front between 8 and 11 March and the obvious and growing threat of an Allied airborne landing led to a considerable strengthening of the anti-aircraft defences. By the time the Allied assault across the Rhine began, there were 814 heavy and light anti-aircraft guns deployed east of the Rhine opposite Second Army and in addition a large number of 13mm anti-aircraft machine guns had been issued to the units of the First Parachute Army.

On the northern flank of the German Rhine defences was General Schlemm's armoured reserve, the XLVII Panzer Corps, positioned near the Dutch frontier. General Freiherr Heinrich von Lüttwitz had led his corps with intiative and drive in the Battle of the Ardenes, but now his two divisions, the 116th Panzer and the 15th Panzer Grenadier, were tired and dispirited and only 35 tanks were still running.

All the German soldiers defending this last ditch knew that the war was lost. Every day and every night they watched the endless procession of Allied bombers droning overhead to smash their cities and their homes; they listened with an ancient Teutonic dread to the news each day of the Russians advancing towards Germany's eastern borders; and they looked in vain for more men, more tanks and more guns. They themselves now began to suffer an ever increasing fury of attack from the air.

By the end of February the troops of the 6th Airborne Division were back from Holland in their camps and billets on Salisbury Plain and General Eric Bols had received from General Ridgway his orders for the Rhine crossing. Planning, briefing and the refurbishing of men and equipment was pressed on in every unit and

on 6 March General Bols summoned his brigade and battalion commanders to Bulford to hear his detailed orders. Wearing battle-dress with his customary hunting stock round his neck, Eric Bols pointed out the task of each brigade on a detailed, large scale model of the division's landing zones and objectives. Round the model were grouped the three brigade commanders and the commander, Royal Artillery and behind them were the battalion commanders, of which I was one, listening intently. Large scale air photographs and maps formed a back-drop to the General's clear and logical outline of the division's tasks and to each brigadier, as he explained in his turn the actions of his battalions. The massive artillery and air support available, the allotment of aircraft and gliders, the estimates of enemy strength and the general impression of a well-organised plan gave us great confidence, even if there remained some slight apprehension at the prospect of jumping directly on top of the enemy's positions.

The two divisions were to fly in side by side, with the British 6th Airborne Division coming from East Anglia on the left and the American 17th on the right, flying from airfields round Paris. The British 3rd and 5th Parachute Brigades

were to land on DZ 'A' and 'B' at the north end of the Diersfordter Wald to destroy the enemy artillery and to clear the northern half of the woods. Close behind them, the gliders of the 6th Airlanding Brigade and divisional troops would land on Landing Zones 'P', 'R', 'O' and 'U'. The 2nd Battalion Oxfordshire and Buckinghamshire Light Infantry or to give them their old number, the 52nd, and the 1st Battalion, Royal Ulster Rifles, were to secure the crossings over the River Issel, while the 12th Battalion, The Devonshire Regiment captured the village of Hamminkeln. Each glider pilot was to land as close as possible to the tactical objective of the troops in his glider.

The six parachute battalions of the British division were to fly in 242 C-47 aircraft of the 61st, 315th and 316th Groups of the US 52nd Wing, flying from Chipping Ongar, Boreham and Wethersfield. The other wings of the IX Troop Carrier Command, the 50th and 53rd, together with the remaining groups of 52 Wing would carry the 17th Airborne Division in 1,155 C-47 and C-46 aircraft and 908 gliders from airfields round Paris. The RAF Stirlings and Halifaxes of 38 Group and the Dakotas of 46 Group had the job of towing the 381 Horsas and Hamilcars for

Below: More C-47's and Waco gliders, marshalled for Operation Varsity. USAAF ground crews in the foreground./*IWM*

Left: The crew of a C-47 discuss the plan with their glider pilots./*IWM*

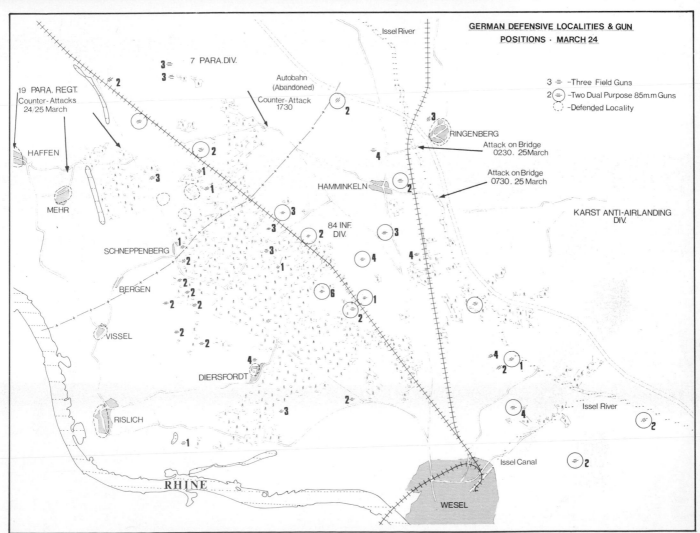

GERMAN DEFENSIVE LOCALITIES & GUN POSITIONS · MARCH 24

Issel River

3 ⇌ 7 PARA. DIV.
3 ⇌

19 PARA. REGT.
Counter-Attacks
24/25 March

2

Autobahn
(Abandoned)
Counter-Attack
1730

2

3 ⇌ –Three Field Guns
2 ⊜ –Two Dual Purpose 85m.m Guns
◯ –Defended Locality

⇌3 RINGENBERG

HAFFEN

2

Attack on Bridge
0230. 25 March

4

MEHR

3

1

2

HAMMINKELN

⊜2

Attack on Bridge
0730. 25 March

KARST ANTI-AIRLANDING
DIV.

1

SCHNEPPENBERG

3

84 INF.
DIV.

3

3

⇌2

3

4

1

4

BERGEN

2
2

2

⊜6

⊜1

⇌2

2

⊜2

VISSEL

2

2

4

⊜1

2

DIERSFORDT

4

4
2

1

2

Issel River

3

RISLICH

4

⇌2

1

Issel Canal

⊜2

WESEL

RHINE

the 6th Airlanding Brigade and the supporting troops of the 6th Division.

These orders sent us all away from that Order Group in a cheerful and confident mood. The three battalion commanders of the 3rd Parachute Brigade, George Hewetson from the 8th, Jeff Nicklin from the Canadians and myself were also privately delighted by the way in which our own brigadier, James Hill, had explained his plan and our tasks, stealing the show by his decisive and eloquent delivery.

Two days later James Hill, Paul Gleadell of the Devons, myself and one or two others were told to report to Netheravon airfield at 8am ready to fly to Rheims, the headquarters of the 17th Airborne Division. We were commanding battalions on the right flank of the British 6th Airborne Division and were to link up with the Americans. Now we were to hear General Miley's orders and meet our opposite numbers. I arrived at the airfield in good time, wearing my best service uniform with our divisional arm badge of

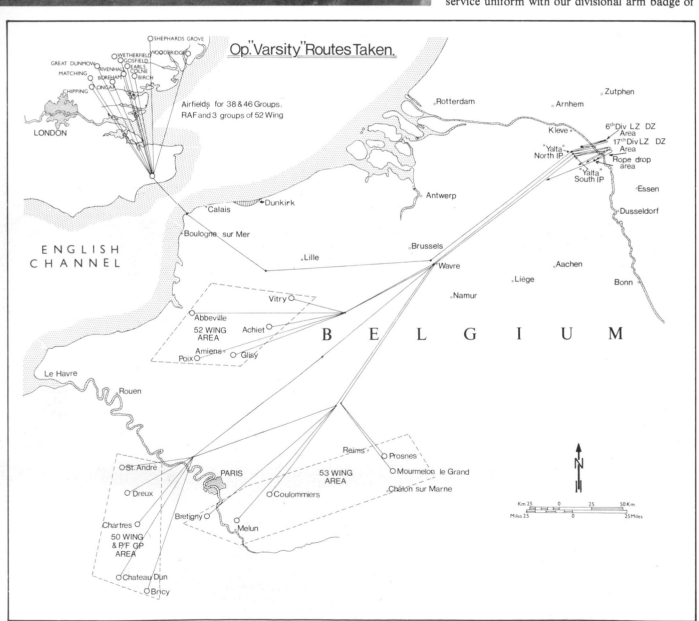

Op."Varsity" Routes Taken.

Airfields for 38 & 46 Groups.
RAF and 3 groups of 52 Wing

Far left, top: RAF Halifax aircraft and Hamilcar gliders, ready for take off at Tarrant Rushton.

Left: A Horsa load of British gunners pose for a picture with the tug aircrew and their two glider pilots./*IWM*

Below: 'Nine-ship elements' of the American IXth Troop Carrier Command over the Channel, carrying men of the British parachute brigades to the Rhine./*IWM*

a blue silk Pegasus on a maroon patch, my red beret and a highly polished Sam Browne belt. This effort to impress the Americans was at once undone by an order to hand in my red beret, and some rapid work on my arm badges by a sergeant with some scissors. Feeling very scruffy with no hat and red thread all over my jacket sleeves, I joined the others in the Dakota to find James Hill sitting there, looking most unusual in a Brigadier's peaked hat with its red band. All this was in the interests of security and to conceal the fact that the two airborne divisions were planning something together.

At Rheims we were led through the commandeered office building, which was General Miley's headquarters, passing many military policemen, clerks, orderlies and staff officers, going about their business very briskly and we were all struck by the Americans' turn-out and bearing and high standard of saluting. This was very different from the customary British view of the happy-go-lucky Yanks.

We were made very welcome and joined the group of American battalion commanders, standing at the back of the briefing room, behind their regimental commanders. Before much the same sort of photographs and maps, as we had seen at Bulford, General Miley gave a brief outline of his plan and then his Chief of Staff filled in the details. Each regimental commander explained how he was to carry out the task set him, just as our own brigadiers had done, with the major difference that the American orders at each level of command were far less detailed. Colonel Edson Raff, commanding the 507th Parachute Infantry, was the shortest speaker of them all. Looking very tough and very square with his crew-cut, he stood up, pointed at the wall-map, and said 'the 507th are flying in west to east and jumping here. We get together here. In these woods are a bunch of Heinies and we sort 'em out'. Then he sat down to a ripple of admiring laughter. The 507th were in fact to drop on the south-west corner of the woods, while the 513th Parachute Infantry's drop zone was just east of the railway. Close by was Landing Zone 'N', where the 17th Division's engineers were to land and in the south east the 194th Glider Infantry were to come down close to the Issel river bridges.

I met Colonel Miller of the 513th's 2nd Battalion, whose final position was to be

Below: Another picture of British parachute troops in an American C-47. The bulge over the stomach is the small pack, carried there for the drop. In front of the man on the right is his No 4 rifle in its felt valise.

Left: Sticks from 3rd Parachute Brigade over DZ 'A'. The far line of parachutes represents a good, regular dropping cadence./*IWM*

Below: British parachute soldiers in a C-47 on the way to Operation Varsity, wearing the standard British X type parachute with its quick-release box over the stomach. Reserve parachutes were only introduced in the British service in 1952./*IWM*

close by the objective of my own 9th Battalion and we arranged how and where we hoped to meet and make contact. After a quick and cheerful lunch party General Miley shook us all by the hand, gave each man a bottle of ex-Luftwaffe brandy and we flew home to Netheravon and our barracks at Bulford. It had been a good day and we were impressed by the Americans.

D-Day for the operation had been set for 24 March with P-hour, the time of the first drop, at 10am. The British 1st Commando Brigade were to cross by boat at 9pm on the previous evening to capture Wesel, in the wake of a heavy air attack on the town by RAF Bomber Command. At 10pm the leading divisions of XII Corps, the 15th Scottish and the 51st Highland, were to begin crossing and it was hoped that the sudden appearance overhead next morning of two complete airborne divisions whould shatter the German Rhine defences.

On 17 March we all moved into transit camps near our take-off airfields in Essex. My own 9th Battalion settled into a disused mushroom farm near Wethersfield, where we were sealed in with barbed wire and all the usual rules of strict security. We set up our models and air photos in a specially guarded room and I gave out my orders to the company commanders. We were to drop last on Drop Zone 'A', after the 8th and Canadian battalions and while they secured the landing area, we were to move southwards to attack and capture the highest part of the Diersfordter Wald, the Schneppenberg, destroying several batteries of German guns on the way.

94

Above left: The leading aircraft of the 6th Airborne Division over Weeze. The US 61st Troop Carrier Group carrying the 8th Parachute Battalion and 3rd Brigade Headquarters and flying from Chipping Ongar./*IWM*

Left: The Prime Minister, Mr Winston Churchill; General Eisenhower and Field Marshal Montgomery watch the crossing on the morning of 24 March./*IWM*

Above: Crews of a British armoured regiment watch the aircraft overhead from their Sherman tanks./*IWM*

Centre right: A 40mm Bofors light anti-aircraft gun crew near Weeze watch the airborne troops go over./*IWM*

Bottom right: German civilians, working for the Allies on road-maintenance, look up at the troop-carriers./*IWM*

Then the whole battalion crowded into the same room, all 600 of them, and I explained our drop and our tasks in some detail. It was both an exhilarating and a sobering experience, talking to so many men of such quality and realising how intently each one of them was following my words and their tasks, as the plan unfolded. I must have spoken for 20 minutes or more with hardly a sound, a cough or a movement from the men. Afterwards each company and each platoon took its turn in the briefing room and each man had to confirm, on the model in front of his own platoon, his rendezvous, his task and the objectives of his company and of the battalion.

Two days before D-Day I went over to Wethersfield to meet our American aircrews and to explain to them our plan and our tasks. Their Colonel said to me in front of them all 'I guess you'll be flying with me in the lead ship' and I had to explain that we allotted sticks and men to aircraft to match their likely landing places on the droping zones and that I planned to jump from the centre of his group in order to be in the middle of the battalion on the ground. I think he thought me windy and he was right to the extent that I had no wish to fly at the very point of this great

wedge of aircraft, a prime target for the German gunners.

On 23 March most men wrote their 'last letters' for posting after the drop, in which they were allowed for the first time to say where they were going. In accordance with normal wartime rules, these letters had to be censored by the company officers — a long, tedious and in many ways a distasteful job, made no better in B Company, by a lance corporal, who turned in no less than eleven last letters to eleven different women, swearing deathless devotion to each of them.

That same night the Allied artillery, 3,500 field, medium and heavy guns, opened fire from their battery positions west of the Rhine against the German defences on the east bank. It was the climax to a tremendous build-up of firepower. As early as 21 February the Allied Air Forces had begun to isolate the battlefield with attacks on airfields, railways, roads and bridges from Bremen down to the Ruhr. In the three days before 24 March, helped by sunshine and clear skies, 3,471 aircraft dropped 8,500 tons of bombs on German roads, railways and airfields and another 2,090 bombers unloaded 6,600 tons on German barracks and military positions. Beneath

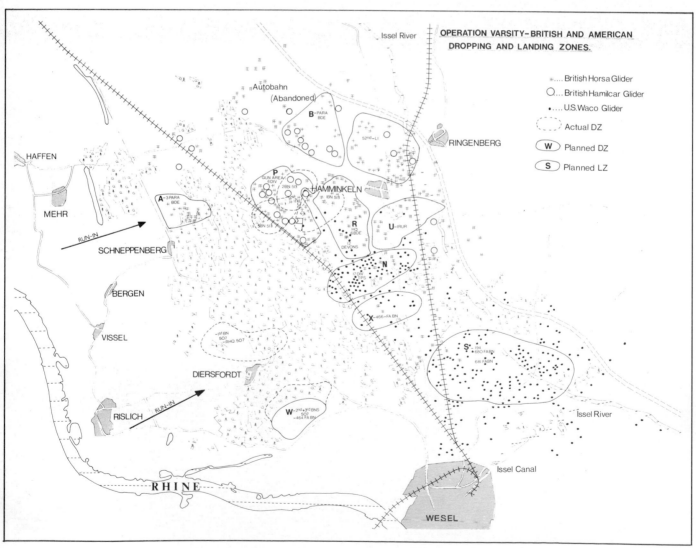

these heavy and medium bombers Allied fighters swept the country east of the Rhine, diving on to anything which moved on the roads and railways with their bombs, cannon and machine guns and attacking each flak battery, as it opened fire — and one of these armed reconnaissance sweeps found the headquarters of First Parachute Army, and severly wounded General Schlemm.

At 9pm on 23 March the Commandos crossed the river in their assault boats and shortly afterwards Bomber Command Lancasters flattened Wesel, sending up a huge cloud of dust and smoke. This mingled with the smoke drifting eastwards from 21 Army Group's 50-mile smoke screen, which had covered the move forward of the assaulting divisions, and caused a good many problems next morning for the Allied fighter pilots seeking to destroy the German anti-aircraft guns, and the glider pilots looking for their landing zones.

At 10pm XII Corps began crossing near Xanten and an hour later XXX Corps took to the water further north. By 4am the American Ninth Army had begun to cross south of Wesel and by dawn 21 Army Group had nine small bridgeheads on the east bank, some of them

under heavy pressure from the German defenders. In England the units of 6th Airborne Division were on their airfields by 5.30am with each parachute stick and glider load beside their aircraft, ready to emplane. It was still dark, but as the light grew we could see it was going to be a fine morning. At Wethersfield I was just getting into a jeep to make a final tour of the battalion's 41 aircraft, lined up nose to tail round the perimeter track, when there was the sound of a shot. A jeep took me down the line to a knot of men near one of the aircraft, where I found a sergeant, lying on the ground, looking ruefully at the ugly mess of his right foot. Another jeep came up and he was whisked away to the Airfield Medical Centre. This was an unexpected blow and a perplexing one, as I could not see how anyone so experienced or with as good a record in action could have been careless enough to let off his rifle or so frightened as to commit the crime of a self-inflicted wound.

However, there was no time to worry about that now, as it was time to emplane. The men climbed in, sat down on the hard metal seats along the side of the fuselage and strapped in. Our American pilots and crew-chief, a senior Warrant

Below: 5.5-inch guns of the 59th Medium Regiment on 23 March ready to open fire on the east bank — typical of the massed artillery available to support the crossing./*IWM*

Officer, came down the fuselage, talking to the men and checked with me 'I'll give a four minute red, OK?' There was a lot of cheerful backchat and then the engines started. Soon we were taxying round towards the runway in a long queue to the sound of 160 Pratt and Whitney engines. I was sitting at the aft end of the stick, opposite the open door and had a good view of take-off. Our C-47 turned on to the runway, lined up with two others in a tight V-formation and all three set off together, the two outside aircraft tucking their wings in behind those of the leader.

Thirtyone minutes later all 80 aircraft from Wethersfield were in the air and forming up into 'nine ship elements', in three vics of three, and then into 'serials' of 40 aircraft each.

The rest of the American aircraft carrying British parachute troops took off without incident and on time, except at Chipping Ongar, where a V.1 buzz-bomb caused some excitement, as it passed overhead just before take-off at nine minutes past seven. At Boreham, the IX Troop Carrier Command report states, 'emplaning was briefly delayed, while the British finished their inevitable tea'.

We left the English coast at Hawkinge and a few minutes later were passing over the bomb-scarred German gun emplacements on Cap Griz Nez. Over Belgium I caught a glimpse of some of the 213 Spitfires from RAF Fighter Command, who were our escort and who were wheeling and zooming above the long train of transports. Our crew chief kept up a cheerful running commentary on the various check-points and sights of interest below and the tea container was passed up and down from man to man. Although the flight was fairly smooth, a few men signalled

Left: Gunners of the 466th Parachute Field Artillery have the usual struggle to get into their equipment and parachute harness, before emplaning in C-47's of the 434th Troop Carrier Group at Mourmelon-le-Grand./*IWM*

Below left: The line-up of C-47's with Wacos each side of them./*IWM*

Right: Men of the 513th Parachute Infantry assembling by their C-46 Commando aircraft at Achiet./*US Army*

Below: . . . and 'emplaning'./*IWM*

for the sick bucket and occasionally someone felt the need to unstrap, unbutton and burrow down through parachute harness, jumping jacket, web equipment, airborne smock and battledress trousers in order to use the urine tin.

At Wavre in Belgium our column turned to the northeast, on course for the Rhine, and joined the 17th Airborne Division aircraft, coming up out of the south west. Looking out of our starboard windows I could see their aircraft and gliders stretching back for miles, while from the door on our port side the parachute aircraft, tug aircraft and gliders of our own division from England were still coming up over the horizon. Ahead the two streams of aircraft, each nine aircraft wide, were flying on, side by side, towards the north east. It was a thrilling sight and a massive demonstration of air power, never likely to be repeated.

There was some singing in the early part of our three hour flight, but most men went to sleep or relapsed into the usual state of half-conscious, suspended animation, until the yell of 'Twenty minutes to go' woke us up and sent the adrenalin pumping through our veins.

Above: One of the direction signs, put out on the west bank of the Rhine for the troop carrier pilots./*IWM*

Top right: A C-47 on fire, after crashing west of the Rhine./*IWM*

Bottom right: View from the cockpit of a Horsa over the second pilot's left shoulder. Two Stirling-Horsa combinations are visible below, all on their way to the Rhine./*IWM*

We were over the battle-scarred wilderness of the Reichswald and the terrible ruins of Goch, when the order 'Stand up! Hook up!' brought us to our feet. Each man fastened the snap-hook on the end of his parachute strop to the overhead cable, fixed the safety pin and turned aft, holding the strop of the man in front in his left hand and steadying himself with his right on the overhead cable. The stick commander, Sergeant Matheson, checked each man's snap hook, we all checked the man in front and beginning with the last man of the stick shouted out in turn 'Number 16 OK — Number 15 OK!' and so on down to myself at Number 1.

Just aft of the door stood the crew chief in his flying helmet and overalls, listening on the intercom for our pilot's orders. I was watching the red and green lights above the door and I am sure the rest of the stick were too. The red light glowed, the crew chief yelled 'Red on. Stand to the door' and I moved forward, left foot first, until I was in the door with both hands holding the door edges, left foot on the sill and the slip stream blasting my face.

Then the great, curving river was below me and seconds later, a blow on the back from the crew chief and a bellow of 'Green On. Go!' in my left ear sent me out into the sunlight. Once the tumbling and jerking were over and my parachute had developed, I had a wonderful view of the dropping zone right below me. I could see the double line of trees along the road on the west and the square wood in the middle of the DZ. The ground was already covered with the parachutes of the 8th and Canadian Battalions and I could see them running towards their objectives. There was a continuous rattle of machine gun fire and the occasional thump of a mortar bomb or a grenade and during my peaceful minute of descent, I heard the crack and thump of two near misses. It was clearly a most accurate and concentrated drop and I felt a surge of confidence and delight.

We had, in fact, reached the Rhine nine minutes early, the only flaw in 52 Wing's performance, but the aircrew had realised this and had given us all the proper warnings. The disadvantage was that the 544 guns firing at the enemy's anti-aircraft guns and the 767 others pounding his defensive positions had to cease fire early, as our aircraft reached the area of their shell trajectories.

General James Gavin, commanding the 82nd Airborne Division, was flying as an observer, well above the incoming transports, and describes the scene in these words:

'It was a new experience to fly an airborne mission, but not jump it. It was an indescribably impressive sight. Three columns, each nine ships or four double-tow gliders across, moved on the Rhine. On the far side of the river it was surprisingly dusty and hazy, no doubt caused by the earlier bombing and artillery fire. On the near bank of the Rhine, clearly visible were panel letters to guide the troop carrier pilots. Yellow smoke was also being used near the panels. It was hard to see how any pilot could make a serious navigational error. The air armada continued on and crossed the river. Immediately it was met by what seemed to me, a terrific amount of flak. A number of ships and gliders went down in flames and after delivering their troops, a surprising number of troop carrier pilots we saw on their way back were flying aircraft that were afire. The crew I was with counted 23 ships burning in sight at one time. But the incoming pilots continued on their course, undeterred by the awesome spectacle ahead.'

Over DZ 'A' 70 of our aircraft were hit by 20mm shells or machine gun bullets and our 316th Group commander's lead aircraft was hit and set on fire, just as the last man jumped. Luckily the crew were all able to bale out safely.

Things were rougher for the 5th Parachute Brigade on Dropping Zone 'B'. Here the Dakotas from Boreham and Wethersfield dropped nearly

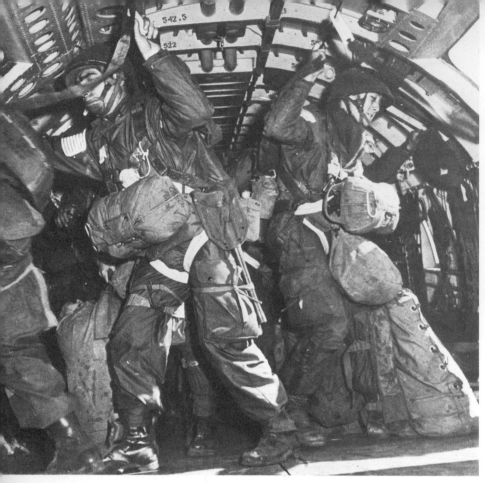

Above: 513th jumping from the double doors of a C-46. Their reserve parachute is on the stomach; they are wearing the British-style harness with a quick-release box instead of the old five-buckle sort. The kit-bag, another British equipment, is strapped to either leg; entrenching tool and waterbottle are visible; and each man is steadying himself with a hand on his strop and on the overhead cable./*IWM*

2,000 men of the 5th Brigade between three and 18 minutes past ten, but they met a lot of flak. Two aircraft were hit and burning as they ran in, but kept a steady course until all had jumped. In other aircraft seven men got tangled in the strops and failed to jump. As the tight formation of 315 Group aircraft banked to port and began their turn for home, they ran into intense light flak from the German 7th Parachute Division in the woods near Mehr. Ten aircraft were shot down in the next minute and crashed east of the Rhine and seven came down in friendly territory west of the river. Seventy more were damaged, six aircrew were killed and 15 wounded in the planes, and 20 were missing.

There was no interference from the Luftwaffe. There had been 80 Me262 jet aircraft on five airfields within range of the airborne landings, but the Allied Air Forces gave them no chance to intervene. 83 and 84 Groups of the RAF flew 900 Spitfire sorties that morning to cover the landings and south of Wesel American fighters from the XXXIX Tactical Air Command kept the skies clear for the US Ninth Army. The only air attacks which failed to achieve their main aim, were the bombers going for the German flak batteries in the area of the airborne landings. Here the smoke, dust and haze prevented the pilots and bomb aimers from getting a clear view of the targets and only half the guns were attacked. Further to the east, beyond Münster, the long range Mustangs of the VIII Air Force made 1,158 sorties and their pilots intercepted two German attempts to attack the Allied

landings, shooting down nearly all the enemy aircraft.

The tug and glider combinations from 38 Group and 46 Group RAF took off at 6am, an hour before the parachute lift, as they took longer to climb to altitude, to form up in their loose pairs and to set course. Only one tug failed to start, but 33 others never reached the Rhine. Sixteen lost control because of air turbulence, nine tow-ropes broke and two gliders ditched in the Channel, where their crews and passengers were picked up by the Air-Sea Rescue service.

The RAF Halifax, Stirling and Dakota crews were briefed to release their gliders over the target area at 2,500 feet, in contrast to the American practice of releasing gliders at 600 feet and this, coupled with the smoke and dust over the landing zones, resulted in only seven RAF aircraft being shot down and 32 damaged. Four hundred and two of the gliders were released at the right place, although a few of them were cast off too high at about 3,500 feet. Visibility was down to about 1,000 yards and the glider pilots' difficulties were increased by intense machine gun and artillery fire from the ground. Ten gliders were shot out of the sky and 284 more were damaged by flak. The gunners on a German 88 on Landing Zone 'P' caused a lot of damage and casualties, as they held their fire until a glider had touched down, traversed round as the glider made its landing run, and then fired, as the glider stopped. Thirty-two gliders were completely destroyed on the ground and 38 more were under such heavy fire that their crews could not unload them.

In spite of these hazards ninety per cent of the Horsas and Hamilcars landed on the correct zones and many of them within a few yards of their objective — a bridge, a farm, a corner of a wood, or a crossroads. In the British landings 38 officers and sergeants of the Glider Pilot Regiment were killed, 77 were wounded and 135 were missing. These were heavy losses, heavier than on the first day at Arnhem or in Normandy and might have been heavier still, if some of the American 513th Parachute Infantry had not been dropped by mistake on Landing Zone 'P' and 'R', and if both the American parachutists and the British glider men had not run straight from their various touch-down points to attack the German gunners.

The 17th Airborne Division airlift began at 7.25am when a C-47 of the Troop Carrier Path Finder Group took off from Chartres. Flying it was Colonel Joel Crouch, who had led the 101st Airborne Division's aircraft into Normandy and who had flown as a pathfinder in Italy, Southern France and Holland. Flying with him was Colonel Edson Raff, leading the 507th Parachute Infantry. Their serial of 46 aircraft were all in the air off one runway in five minutes and only ten minutes later they swept over the airfield, already closed up in their tight formation of 'nine-ship elements'.

The crews of IX Troop Carrier Command were by now a well-disciplined, highly professional and experienced bunch, and although this particular group was probably one of the best, all of them could fly these tight, precise formations and knew the importance of a steady platform for their jumpers and an accurate and consistent tow for their gliders.

Each aircrew member wore armour — flak helmet, flak vest, flak apron over the legs and a flak pan to sit on. He was armed with a trench knife and a Thompson sub-machine gun, a carbine or a Colt .45 pistol and each aircraft carried hand grenades. Most of the C-47s had by now been fitted with self-sealing fuel tanks, but they were still vulnerable to ground weapons, particularly as they ran in to a drop zone or a landing zone on a straight and level course at 110mph and only 600 feet above the ground. Operation Varsity was the culmination of a lot of flying and the American orders for it included the recommendation of each serial leader for the American Distinguished Flying Cross and of each aircrew member for the Air Medal.

In these aircraft of IX Troop Carrier Command were thirteen war correspondents from the *New York Times*, the *Chicago Tribune*, Mutual Broadcasting Company, the National Editorial Association, Associated Press, the *Air Force Magazine*, the French News Service, *Stars and Stripes* and the Columbia Broadcasting Service. Two of them jumped with the parachute regiments and Richard C. Hottelet from CBS, with Sergeant Fred W. Quandt, a photographer,

flew in a B-17 Flying Fortress, watching and photographing the drop from above. Minutes after Quandt had taken the photograph on page 78 the aircraft was hit by flak. Hottelet, Quandt and ten other men in the crew were ordered to bale out and all but one got safely down — Quandt with his camera and films. Technical Sergeant Clarence A. Pearce of the Command Public Relations Branch was killed, as his parachute failed to open fully. The pilot, Lieutenant Colonel Benton R. Baldwin, stayed with the aircraft, although one wing was on fire, and brought it down to a belly-landing west of the Rhine.

All the way to the Rhine the 181 Dakotas carrying the 507th Parachute Infantry and 464th Parachute Field Artillery Battalion flew in perfect order and fine weather, following their ace pathfinder, Colonel Crouch. Their objective was DZ 'W', some open fields on the south edge of the Diersfordter Wood about two and a half miles or one and a half minutes' flying time beyond the Rhine. The DZ was about 2,000 yards long and a mile wide and the Alter Rhein, the old course of the river, now a long, finger-shaped lake, pointed directly at the DZ. It was unmistakeable, but as Crouch came over the river at the point of his flying wedge of 46 Dakotas, he could see nothing but a pall of smoke. Exactly ninety seconds later at 9.50am he switched on the green jump light, his crewman flashed a green lamp from the astrodome to the formation behind and out went Colonel Raff and the men of the 1st Battalion. They hit the ground in open fields just north of Diersfordt village and castle and about two miles

Above: A C-47 tows off two Waco gliders, probably from 446 Group at Melun./*IWM*

north west of the right DZ 'W' The 438th Group from Prosnes dropped the 2nd and 3rd Battalions right on DZ 'W', together with the gunners, although a few of the latter were dropped wide in the woods to the north. Jumping with the artillery was General Miley and a small staff and his headquarters was soon functioning in its chosen spot at the south-east end of the woods.

The 513th Parachute Infantry and their gunners, the 466th Parachute Field Artillery were to drop on DZ 'X', an area of small flat fields, divided by wooden fences just beyond the double track railway running north from Wesel on the east side of the Diersfordter woods. It was five miles or three minutes beyond the Rhine. They were to fly in only 72 of the big, new C-46 Curtis Commando aircraft which could carry twice the load of a C-47 and provided jump doors on both sides of the fuselage. They cruised faster too and were timed to overtake the slower formation of C-47. The two serials of C-46s were scheduled to reach Wavre at 9.34am and 9.38am, fly up the left hand stream, temporarily clear of British planes, and pass the leading American glider formation, due at Wavre at 9.36am. As they approached Wavre, the faster C-46s saw the glider column crossing in front of them, so while the leading C-46s swung left, outpaced the glider train and swung back into line ahead of them, the second serial of C-46s climbed up to 2,000 feet and flew over the top of the glider stream — the whole movement typical of the complicated but carefully calculated flight plans for these swarms of aircraft and the quick thinking and disciplined flying needed to solve these instant problems.

As they flew over the Rhine only one crew reported seeing the marker panels laid out on the west bank and east of the river they could only see it for about half a mile owing to the same dust and smoke, which were hampering the other formations. There was some light flak now and by the time they were over the woods, two aircraft were burning. No one bailed out and both aircraft flew on steadily to drop their parachutists. As they came down to 600 feet, they were hit by intense and accurate light flak and machine gun fire and the sky seemed suddenly full of burning and exploding planes. Those beautiful, tight formations began to break up and pilots had to bank and turn to avoid collisions or slow down to near stalling speed. One C-46 stalled and fell out of the sky with all its crew and parachutists on board. Sixty-eight other aircraft dropped their men accurately, as they thought, but in fact the three battalions landed in a dispersed pattern all over the British landing zones 'P' and 'R', two miles north of their proper Drop Zone 'X'.

The hail of 20mm shells and machine gun bullets continued, until the aircraft had turned to starboard over the River Issel and begun their flight home to Achiet. Most of them got back there between 11.10 and 11.47, but 19 planes had been destroyed by the German anti-aircraft gunners and 38 more were badly damaged. One crew-man was killed in his aircraft, 22 more were wounded and 33 were missing. Fourteen of these new C-46s had gone down in flames and there was much talk about the cause of this weakness, some thinking it the complicated hydraulic system and others blaming the arrangement of the fuel tanks in the wings.

For some hours after the drop Colonel Coutts had no contact with his gunners, who were nowhere to be seen. In fact forty-five C-47s of 434th Group from Mourmelon Le Grand had dropped all the gunners and their 12 howitzers accurately on DZ 'X', except for nine over-eager men, who had jumped too early and landed west of the Rhine.

The 194th Glider Infantry, two artillery battalions and the 17th Divisional engineers, signals and support troops were to take off from the 50th and 53rd Wing airfields south of Paris. The aircraft of four groups were each towing two gliders carrying the 194th and the 680th and 681st Field Artillery to Landing Zone 'S' in the angle of the River Issel and the Issel Canal, two miles north east of Wesel. In three of these glider pairs the tow-ropes fouled, causing two fatal crashes. The after-action report on one of them reads — '40mins out from A55 (Melun) one wing came off, glider cut loose, other fell off before it hit ground. All killed. Load lost'. Air turbulence was bad and 18 other gliders had to cast off prematurely and failed to reach the battle.

All the gliders met the problem of smoke and dust over the landing zones, but very few pilots went off course. During the run-in to LZ 'S' two tugs were shot down and as the fire from the ground got worse, after they had released their gliders, ten more were destroyed and another 140 damaged before they reached the Rhine on the return journey.

The last, seven American serials, flying to Landing Zone 'N' with the divisional troops, were equally successful. Out of 313 aircraft flying over the LZ only three were lost and 44 damaged and nearly all the gliders were released at the right place.

It had been a successful day for the RAF's 38 and 46 Groups and for the US IX Troop Carrier Command. The two RAF Groups had achieved a 92% success rate for the loss of only seven tugs and 27 aircrew. American aircraft had dropped 8,677 men and released over the landing zones 883 gliders out of the 908 which had started. They had lost 58 planes shot down, 352 had been damaged and their casualties in aircrew were eight dead and 108 missing.

Losses in glider pilots and gliders were much more severe, as they released from their tugs and dived down into the smoke and dust of the battlefield. Most of the German gun crews were quick to realise the threat of these gliders, silently descending on them through the haze, and they made the most of such rewarding targets.

The British 6th Airborne in Action

The 8th Parachute Battalion, led by a short, square Cumberland schoolmaster, George Hewetson, had the job of clearing the dropping zone of the enemy, dug in round it. Each company ran from their parachutes straight to their objectives; B Company and the machine gun platoon to the small square wood projecting from the south side of the DZ; A Company against another small wood on the north east corner; and C Company with battalion headquarters and the mortars to the triangular wood on the south east corner. This corner was also the rendezvous for the 9th Battalion and brigade headquarters and a special party jumped from the leading aircraft to mark it with blue smoke.

George Hewetson landed fifty yards away from the square wood in the middle of the DZ and stood for a moment to watch the ordered mass of Dakotas flying overhead amid the smoke puffs of bursting shells, the lazy-looking streams of red tracer shells curving up towards them, the mass of 9th Battalion parachutes still coming down and a Dakota banking away to the north with a wing on fire. Bullets were whipping across the DZ and he became aware of a lot of fire from the square wood, which was B Company's objective.

This was held by two platoons of the German 7th Parachute Division and they were making a fight of it. Major Kippin and one of his platoons attacked through the woods from the south, but were beaten back with both Kippin and the platoon commander shot dead. The wounded lying out in the open were under fire and the stretcher bearers of the field ambulance had a busy time. One of them, Private Wright, was shot through the head while bringing in a wounded man, and the brigade dentist, Captain Chaundy, doubling as an anaesthetist, stopped near the

Below: Dropping Zone 'A', used by the 3rd Parachute Brigade — a photo used in planning and briefing./*IWM*

Above: Lieutenant Colonel George Hewetson, who led the 8th Parachute Battalion from September 1944 to the end of the war — a schoolmaster and wrestler from Cumberland.

Above right: A British parachute soldier — the coloured strip on the shoulder strap of his airborne smock indicates his battalion: maroon for the 9th, blue for the 8th and so on. He is carrying Sten gun magazines in a webbing bandolier./*IWM*

Right: A C-47 coming down on fire over DZ 'A'.

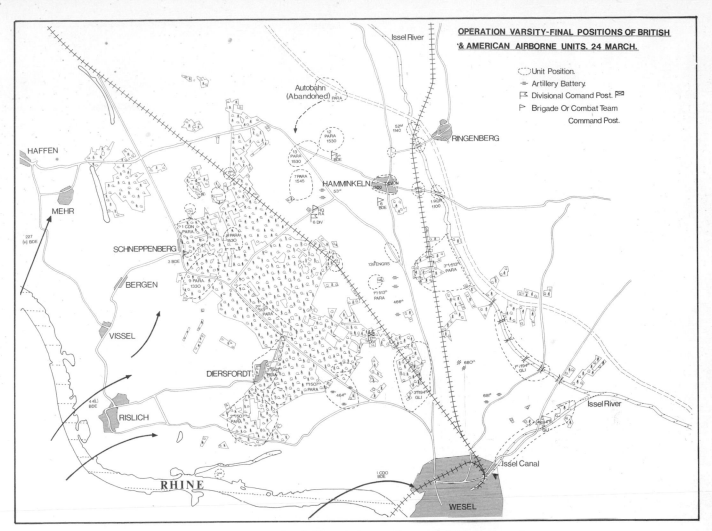

same wood to give first aid to a wounded man. He too was killed. Finally some more of B Company rushed the wood from the DZ covered by fire from the south. Using smoke and 36 Grenades — the Mills Bomb of World War 1 — they killed a number of the enemy and captured an officer and 26 men. In the wood they found the trenches choked with German dead and wounded and several British soldiers hanging dead in the trees, one of them caught by a leg in the branches, head downwards, with a hand outstretched, as if for help. The rest of the battalion occupied their two woods with little trouble, as most of the German defenders had left their trenches and gone forward to meet the British brigades attacking over the Rhine.

The Canadians jumped four minutes after the 8th Battalion and cleared the woods on the south west side of the dropping zone without much trouble. The north side of the dropping zone was also held by men of the German 7th Parachute Division, who put up a stiff resistance and shot several Canadians as they came down and were caught up in the trees. Amongst the men killed this way was Jeff Nicklin, the Canadian commanding officer, whose massive frame was found hanging from a tree, still in his parachute harness, right over a German slit trench. The Catholic padre, Captain Kenny and two men of

the field ambulance, Corporal Nicholson and Driver Shelton, all lost their lives in the same way.

The German parachute troops held out for some time in the houses on the road, north of the woods, and kept up a vigorous fire with mortars and machine guns on the Canadian positions and over the western part of the DZ. Two medical orderlies ran out to a wounded man lying in the open beside a carrier, but both were killed as they knelt beside him. Corporal Topham of the Canadians saw this and in the words of his Victoria Cross citation 'went forward through intense fire to replace the orderlies, who had been killed before his eyes. As he worked on the wounded man, he himself was shot through the nose. In spite of severe bleeding and intense pain, he never faltered in his task. Having completed first aid, he carried the wounded man steadily and slowly back through continuous fire to the shelter of the woods. Refusing help, he continued to perform his duties for two hours, until all casualties had been evacuated from his area. Then, having resisted orders for his own removal, he rescued three men from a burning carrier at great risk from exploding ammunition.'

Last to jump of the three battalions in the 3rd Brigade was my own, the 9th. I landed almost in the middle of the dropping zone with a reasonable forward roll, banged my quick release box, and

Above: Some of the officers of the 8th Battalion. Major Bobbie Gordon, Brigade Major of 3rd Parachute Brigade, Major Archie Bookless the Adjutant, Lieut. Colonel George Hewetson, Major John Kippen B Company, the second in command Major John Tilley, Major Bob Flood A Company and Major John Shappee, C Company./*IWM*

Right: Major Kippen at the door of a C-47./*IWM*

got up. I could see the blue smoke going up at our rendezvous in the far corner of the woods and a lot of men were already moving towards it. The square wood to my right was clearly the centre of a small battle, but all I cared about was getting to our rendezvous. Lance Corporal Wilson, my batman, and CSMI Harrold, our physical training instructor and now my bodyguard, were nowhere to be seen, although they had jumped immediately behind me.

A few minutes later I reached our rendezvous. The Regimental Sergeant Major, Dusty Miller, was standing by his blue smoke canister, grinnning broadly and directing the men to their company locations in a tight circle round the rendezvous. I wanted to get the mortars into action, before we moved off, to cover our advance through the woods to the Schneppenberg and I grabbed a passing mortarman to ask him, where was Alan Jefferson, the Mortar officer. 'He's copped it, sir', was the reply, 'hit in the head and a terrible mess he was'. Five seconds later Alan Jefferson, who had been a ballet dancer, came bouncing by, saluted me and said 'Good morning sir. What a lovely day!' and I sent him hurrying on to get his mortars going.

Wilson now appeared, leading two horses, which he had liberated from a nearby farm, one for me and one for himself, and each company commander reported that the men were coming in well. After 30 minutes we were already 300 strong and a quarter of an hour later we were almost at full strength. Close to my position and

just inside the wood were George Hewetson and his 8th Battalion headquarters. I was standing at the edge of the wood, looking out over the dropping zone, when our gliders appeared overhead and released from their tugs. One of them, a Horsa, misjudged his height and speed and came whistling in, past our corner of the woods and hit the trees right over George's headquarters party. It must have been flying at 80 to 90 knots and broke up with a great, splintering crash. We ran over, to find that it was our own 9th Battalion medical glider. My Medical Sergeant Millot and his two orderlies were dead; their jeep and trailer, full of medical stores, were smashed; the 8th Battalion's Intelligence Officer, England and two of their sergeants had been killed and George was crawling out from under the wreckage, alive but badly bruised.

The battalion were now ready to move and I walked down through the woods for a few hundred yards to report to Brigadier James Hill. Seizing me by the elbow, he said how well everything was going and told me to move as soon as possible for the Schneppenberg. We set off with Alan Parry and his A Company in the lead. Then came Wilson and I on horseback and the rest of battalion headquarters, followed by B and C Companies. After only a few hundred yards we came out into a clearing and saw the wreck of a Horsa glider, lying on its back with most of the fuselage torn open. Inside were a jeep and six-pounder anti-tank gun, with three gunners lying dead beneath the wreckage.

Above: German prisoners being brought in by men of the 1st Canadian Parachute Battalion.

Left: Lieut. Colonel Napier Crookenden, commanding the 9th Battalion taken a few days after the drop on the advance across Germany./*IWM*

109

A Company brushed aside small groups of Germans, mostly from the 84th Division and were soon on the Schneppenberg. On reaching the main road, I dismounted and continued on foot with CSMI Harrold, thinking that B Company had gone on ahead of us to clear our final objective — the western edge of the woods and a German battery there, which we could hear firing. Next minute a machine gun opened fire on us from 50 yards up the track and we took cover behind two trees. Harrold urged me to join him in a two-man, right-flanking assault on the enemy ahead but I preferred to wait for B Company. A few minutes later their leading platoon came up, followed by the rest of the company and the enemy ahead melted away. Harrold, I felt, never again thought very highly of my military valour.

We followed B Company into a German battery of 76mm guns, firing from the western edge of the woods against the 15th Scottish Division, advancing from the Rhine, and in a few minutes of shooting and shouting the Germans were all dead or prisoners. One of our men took a fine pair of binoculars from the neck of a dead German Captain, gave them to me and I have used them ever since.

By 1pm we were dug in on our final positions with A Company on the Schneppenberg, B Company astride the main road to the south east and C Company in the wood, south of the road. Half an hour later a German assault gun on its tracked chassis attacked up the road, accompanied by a few, brave infantrymen and rattled on right into B Company headquarters. Everyone dived for the road ditches, except for the Company clerk, who jumped up, as the gun passed him and banged a Gammon bomb on to the engine covers. The gun stopped, the hatch opened, a crewman looked out and was shot and the rest surrendered. The gun was still a runner and, manned by two ex-tank drivers in B Company, rumbled along behind B Company for the next week of rapid movement.

Top: George Hewetson of the 8th Battalion tries out his wrestling on Fraser Eadie, who took over command of the 1st Canadian Parachute Battalion, after Jeff Nicklin was killed./*IWM*

Above: A Hamilcar glider and its load, a Bren-gun carrier. One was allotted to each parachute battalion for collecting stores.

Right: An 8 Battalion group — Captain Webb, a Canadian; Major Charles Dumbar, who took over B Company after Kippen's death; Major Bob Flood, A Company and Major John Shappee, C Company. /*IWM*

110

During the afternoon James Hill came round to see us and visited each company and later in the evening I was standing by the road, when a jeep drove up, flying a Union Jack on the bonnet and carrying Field Marshal Montgomery. I saluted, explained our situation and advised him to go no further, as we were the sharp end and so far had made no contact with the Americans who should have been in the woods to the south of us. 'Good! Good!', he said, and drove back up the road. That same night he took the trouble to write a Field Service postcard to my father, a retired Colonel living in Berkshire, saying he had seen me alive and well — a thoughtful act by an Army Group Commander on the first evening of a major battle.

Soon after Monty's visit Harrold and I went south into the woods and found the 513th's 2nd Battalion, with whom we were supposed to link up. We had a cheerful talk and some whisky with Miller and his people who had been dropped on the wrong drop zone amongst our gliders and had

had a fairly difficult day, clearing the woods and reaching their final objective. I liked his whisky, but we all preferred our 24-hour ration packs to their K-ration.

The Canadians had cleared Bergerfurth by midday and the 224th Parachute Field Ambulance moved down to set up their main dressing station in the church and the priest's house. The church was full of fallen plaster, splintered pews and smashed saints, so they decided to use it only for reception and minor treatment. Thirty German prisoners were put to work, clearing out the rubble and digging trenches round the church, and the cooks set up shop in an out-building, collecting rations from the wounded and brewing up that famous medicine — hot, sweet tea. The sergeant major went round putting up neat signs, and the surgical teams set to work, transforming the priest's kitchen and living room into an operating theatre and a post-operative room. Coal scuttles, crockery, dirty dishes and broken glass were

Below: A British ambulance jeep brings in two stretcher cases.

Above: Two orderlies from the Royal Army Medical Corps with two prisoners, one Luftwaffe and one Volksturm, employed on digging shelter trenches at the Bergerfurth dressing station./*IWM*

Centre left: A British Medical officer treating a German soldier.

Bottom left: A severely wounded man with a blood plasma drip at Bergerfurth./*IWM*

Top right: Two men of a British glider unit wait outside a dressing station./*IWM*

Bottom right: A medical orderly supervises the moving of German wounded near Bergerfurth./*IWM*

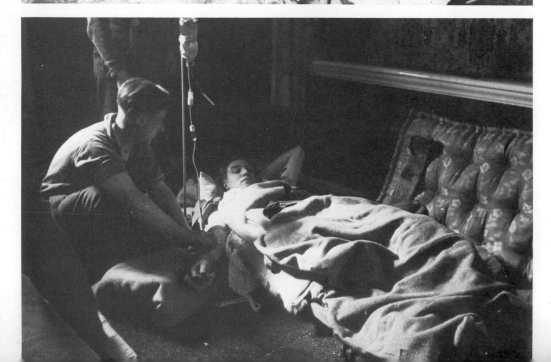

thrown out of the window and two heavy cupboards full of school-books were dragged out of the front door. 'The owner' as the field ambulance record puts it, 'in his black, clerical hat, moved gloomily about the house, searching for valuables among the rubbish and getting in the way.'

At 2.30pm the first patient was on the operating table. Ready-sterilised instruments, pentothal, ether and chloroform, penicillin, sulphanilamide and all the necessary kit for major operations had been dropped on the men, with reserve supplies coming in by glider and each man in the field ambulance headquarters had jumped with a bottle of plasma. In the next 45 hours the two surgeons, Majors Daintree-Johnson and Miller, each did fourteen major operations in the priest's house, all of them too serious to await evacuation over the Rhine. Twenty-three survived. Fifteen of the men had multiple wounds and their injuries from bullets, shells and mortar bombs included six stomach wounds, five fractured thighs, two chest wounds, four amputations and three broken legs.

While this was going on in Bergerfurth at the main dressing station, other men of the field ambulance were scouring the drop zone and the woods near-by for British and German wounded and bringing them in by stretcher, jeep and farm cart. The whole field ambulance, doctors, medical orderlies and drivers, were a remarkable group of men and the knowledge that they were there had a marked effect on the fighting spirit of the battalions.

5th Parachute Brigade's drop on DZ 'B' was equally successful. The three battalions, 7th, 12th and 13th, met only moderate opposition and were soon in position once they had rallied. They took some time to do this as many officers and men found difficulty in deciding where they were, and they were not using any visible markings for their rallying points. One German gunner kept his 88mm firing from the autobahn for a good ninety minutes before he was scuppered, and Lieutenant Burkinshaw with some men of the 13th Battalion captured a troop of four 88mm guns on the DZ.

Far left, top: The three battalion commanders of 5th Brigade on DZ 'B' in 1970 — Geoffrey Pine-Coffin, 7th; Peter Luard, 13th; and Ken Darling, 12th.

Far left, bottom: Another in Hamminkeln station. The tail, upside down, can be seen on the right. Beyond the trees are two more Horsas. All these gliders, carrying battalion headquarters, were briefed to land as close as possible to the station!/*IWM*

Above: A 52rd Light Infantry Horsa, crashed in Hamminkeln station./*IWM*

Centre left: A platoon of the Royal Ulster Rifles digging in on the east bank of the River Issel./*IWM*

Bottom left: A 6-pounder anti-tank gun of the Ulsters, covering one of the Issel bridges./*IWM*

In the gap between the 3rd and 5th Brigades a platoon of the 7th Battalion, led by a Canadian, Lieutenant Patterson, had a lively day in their outpost position on the railway as groups of the German 7th Parachute Division tried to attack them. If the attack was a weak one, Patterson let them come on to close range and then drove them off with rapid fire from his light machine guns and rifles. If it looked like a more determined affair, he withdrew into the woods to a flank, let the Germans deliver their attack on empty trenches and then led his platoon back in a fierce charge, just as the Germans were relaxing. In the brigade that day there were some 300 casualties in killed and wounded, including Pine-Coffin, commanding the 7th Battalion, painfully shot through the nose, but by nightfall they were well dug in and ready for the next day's advance.

In Normandy the parachute brigades had experienced a scattered, rough and costly drop,

Top left: A crashed Hamilcar and a Horsa beyond its nose on LZ 'P'. /IWM

Bottom left: More like the Devons' usual, workmanlike form — a section clearing the village./IWM

Above: A Devons' 6-pounder in Hamminkeln — very much a posed picture and quite unlike their normal positions, dug in and well camouflaged./IWM

Centre right: Hugh Bellamy, commanding the 6th Airlanding Brigade, talking to Major Eddie Warren of the 12th Battalion, the Devonshire Regiment, in Hamminkeln. Warren was one of the survivors of the Battle of Breville in Normandy.

Bottom right: Prisoners of war in a farm near Hamminkeln, watched by a glider soldier from the cart seat./IWM

Right: A Horsa on the ground with flaps fully down. Two American Wacos coming in to land near Hamminkeln./*IWM*

Below: Horsas and Wacos on LZ 'U' south of Hamminkeln./*IWM*

Far right, top: Two British soldiers in the wreckage of a Hamilcar on LZ 'P', watch men of the American 513th moving across the landing zone./*IWM*

Far right, bottom: A Hamilcar on LZ 'P'.

while the glider brigade's landing in the evening of D-Day had been accurate and with very few casualties. Now the picture was reversed. As the gliders dived down into the gloom, they came under intense and accurate fire from the Germans on the landing zones. The 52nd Light Infantry were over LZ 'O' at about 10.30am. Most of the glider pilots caught sight of Hamminkeln church spire and the autobahn and 53 of their 58 gliders landed on the right place. The four gliders of C Company touched down beside the single cantilever girder bridge, which carried the railway over the River Issel and B Company's four did the same at the hump-backed road bridge 300 yards to the south. The air was full of shell-bursts and the red streams of tracer. Gliders were landing and crashing every few seconds and there was a continuous din, made up of the sharp crack of 88mm guns, the banging of 20mm cannon and the rattle of machine guns.

Squadron Leader Reynolds, an RAF officer commanding F Squadron of the Glider Pilot Regiment, was flying a Horsa with Lieutenant Colonel Mark Darell-Brown, his jeep and trailer and some men of battalion headquarters. He was aiming for the railway station, but quadruple 20mm guns in the station were firing at them and scoring hits on the Horsa and the jeep inside it. As they dived down, the second pilot opened fire with his Sten gun through the front perspex and

they landed safely, right beside the German guns.
In a few seconds they were all out and the
German gun crew were dead, wounded or
prisoners. In the station was a goods train, half
full of ammunition and petrol, and ahead of it the
lines were blocked by two locomotives,wrecked
by air attack. Another glider came whistling in
over their heads and smashed into the ground at
high speed, disintegrating into a mass of
splintered wreckage across the railway line.

Major Aldworth, the battalion quartermaster
in another Horsa making for the station, saw that
both his glider pilots had been killed by a burst of
20mm. He dragged one of them back into the
fuselage and, slipping into his seat, landed the
Horsa safely, although he had never flown before.
Captain Bousfield's A Company glider, on its
landing run, cannoned into a German half-track,
which promptly became part of A Company's
transport. Many other gliders, carrying jeeps,
ammunition and petrol, caught fire on being
hit by shells or tracer bullets.

Staff Sergeant Andrews who had already won
a Distinguished Flying Medal, was piloting a
Horsa of A Company. As he released the tow-
rope, an 88mm shell burst close alongside them,
wounding his second pilot in the leg. Andrews
picked up the autobahn, but then found that half-
flap and then full-flap had little effect on his
airspeed, as he approached the LZ. Still flying at
100mph he saw a field ahead, surrounded by tall
poplars and lifted his Horsa over them,
minipulating his flaps as he did so. Ahead of him
the wing of a crashed Horsa stood up vertically
from the ground and Andrews yawed sharply to
avoid it. His starboard wing caught it, his glider
cart-wheeled into the ground and Andrews was
thrown out through the perspex nose. The glider
was completely smashed and several of the men
in it ended up lying on the ground with bits of
their seats still strapped to them.

As all these gliders were landing, three
German tanks and a motor-
cycle drove over the landing

zone from the west, firing as they went, until they ran into the 6-pounder anti-tank guns of the Royal Ulster Rifles further south and were knocked out. By 11.40 Darell-Brown could report to his brigadier that all objectives were taken and the battalion were digging in round the two bridges over the river, the railway station and the road junctions to the west. They were now only 226 in strength, with four mortars instead of 12 and very few anti-tank guns. No less than 103 of the battalion were dead, mostly in the gliders.

In the evening a German patrol came over the autobahn embankment and were chased off by Lieutenant Stone's platoon, who killed two and captured two more. At midnight an attack by infantry and tanks came in from Ringenberg against B Company's road bridge and overran one of B Company's sections just east of the river. The 6-pounders missed the tanks, but Lieutenant Clarke led a charge over the bridge and regained the lost trenches. Two hours later the Germans tried again and this time the bridge was blown up on the orders of the brigadier, Hugh Bellamy.

On Landing Zone 'U', south east of Ringenberg, 59 gliders carrying the Royal Ulster Rifles reached the right place and seven gliders going for the bridges over the railway and the river put their men down within a few yards of each bridge. In 15 minutes the Irishmen were moving to their objectives and had got them all by 11am. One of their 6-pounders came into action, as soon as it had been unloaded, and knocked out two armoured cars from 116 Panzer Reconnaissance Battalion on the landing zone. Another of their Horsa gliders was hit by tracer shells and set on fire in the air, and the starboard

main plane was blown off while they were 50 feet up. The glider pilots got it down to a rough landing and to the surprise of the men watching, the occupants climbed out, bruised but intact.

The Devons' job was to clear Hamminkeln by landing three companies on the west, north and south sides of the village. The fourth company, C, landed half a mile to the west and were to seize Kopenhof Farm for divisional headquarters. Landing with the battalion on LZ 'R' was brigade headquarters and 83 out of 94 gliders reached the Landing Zone.

Lieutenant Colonel Paul Gleadell, the Devons' commanding officer, flew in Horsa No 188 and sat on the first seat on the starboard side. Next to him was his soldier servant, Private Jolly, and opposite him Lieutenant Brixey, the Itelligence Officer. With them were Private Bray from the Intelligence Section and a regimental policeman, Private Tremeer. Lashed in the middle of the glider were the Colonel's jeep and trailer. Major Priest, their first pilot, identified the Issel and the autobahn and, as he cast off the tow and the noise of flight suddenly quietened, shells from 88mm guns and 20mm cannon rocked the glider. Two bursts of machine gun fire came up through the glider floor, wounding Tremeer in the back. Priest shouted 'I can't see a damned thing but I'll do the best I can for you.' There was a crash, the floorboards were torn up, their feet dragged along the earth and Tremeer was hurled against the forward bulkhead, as the glider stopped with a jolt.

Brixey jumped out with a Bren gun and flung himself down to cover the rest, as they scrambled out and fell into a large bomb crater. Bullets were cracking overhead from three directions and a 20mm gun opened fire on them from the autobahn embankment, a hundred yards away. A

Above: A Devons' Horsa: Hamminkeln church in the background.

Left: A British Horsa landing over the heads of men of the 513th, as they move to assemble on LZ 'P'. /*IWM*

Top right: A soldier snatches some sleep./*IWM*

Centre right: Two glider pilots talking to the crew of two scout cars from the 6th Guards Tank Brigade near Bergerfurth after the link-up./*IWM*

Bottom right: A British glider pilot escorting a column of prisoners, mostly Luftwaffe and some Volksturm. Two Horsas in the background./*IWM*

shout in English from the other direction turned their heads. It was a platoon of the 52nd, already digging in on the banks of the River Issel. Gleadell's glider had landed well off their LZ and east of the river, so they set off towards Hamminkeln, his main objective, as fast as they could. On the way they saw many crashed gliders and a number of small battles, as groups of men attacked the Germans, holding out in practically every farm.

Only two platoons of C Company reached Kopenhof Farm. The third platoon, led by Lieutenant Slade, suffered a direct hit on their glider, soon after casting off, and were not seen again. Major Palmer in D Company's headquarters glider had to return to base with a frayed tow-rope. On setting off again, the rear-gunner of their tug aircraft tested his guns so carelessly, that some of his bullets shattered the perspex canopy of the Horsa cockpit, causing a stream of the choicest glider pilot invective to flow over the glider-tug telephone cable. B Company's commander, Major Barrow, was in a Horsa hit by 20mm fire as it came in to land. It crashed east of the River Issel and all on board were killed except Barrow, who was wounded and captured.

Another company commander, Major Rogers, was flown by Captain Boucher-Giles, a veteran of Sicily, Normandy and Arnhem. They flew all the way from base in the low-tow position to avoid turbulance and with the tug nicely framed in the upper half of the cockpit perspex. They saw the Rhine and some parachutes on DZ 'A' and then got the word from the tug to release. They were at 3,200 feet. Boucher-Giles spotted the Issel and the autobahn and knew he was too far east. As he made a steep turn to starboard, machine gun bullets came through the floor and his flaps

123

seemed to be inoperable. He came down to 500 feet in a series of S-turns and then made a good landing in a ploughed field, some 60 yards from the woods and half a mile south of the LZ, among a number of American Waco gliders.

They got out to find themselves under fire from a large building 80 yards away. While Company Sergeant Major Mashford opened up on the farm with a Bren gun, the rest of them set about unloading the glider. As Boucher-Giles was fixing the explosive cord round the tail to blow it off, he was hit in the leg and his second pilot, Sergeant Garland, dragged him into a ditch. They were now under attack by a German tank with some infantry in two half-tracks. Major Rogers was wounded in the arm, Mashford was killed instantly, but they were able to knock out the tank and the half-tracks with a Piat. The two glider pilots were eventually picked up and taken to a medical dressing station by some Americans and the rest of them were able to rejoin the Devons in Hamminkeln.

On Landing Zone 'R' the pioneer platoon's glider was set on fire as it landed. Their officer, Lieutenant Cox, crawled out of the wreckage, only to be knocked down and killed by another Horsa on its landing run. Lieutenant Whiteway's platoon in B Company landed within yards of a farm, full of Germans, firing away as fast as they could and Whiteway was wounded while still in the glider. Sergeant Higginson got the men out, but was killed as he went back inside to get the handcart. The rest of the platoon stormed the

farm and drove out the enemy. By 1pm Hamminkeln had been captured and the battalion were holding it firmly. Five hundred of the garrison were prisoners and turned out to be a very mixed lot — parachute troops, anti-aircraft gunners, Waffen-SS, Volksturm and men from the Karst Battle Group, who had manned most of the 20mm guns.

By nightfall all was quiet round Hamminkeln. The Devons had lost 110 killed and 30 wounded, but like the other two glider battalions, they were pleased with their rapid victory and very ready to press on to the east next morning against a shaken enemy.

Just to the west of the glider battalions and closer to the woods the gunners of the 53rd Light Regiment landed on LZ 'P'. Organised in two batteries of 12 guns each, they had a rough landing and by evening had only been able to collect half their guns. The Forward Observer Battery, a group of forward observer officers and signallers, were quickly into action and through on the radios to the massed artillery on the west bank of the Rhine. Eight massive Hamilcar gliders brought in the Locust light tanks of the Airborne Armoured Reconnaissance Regiment, but only four survived a series of crash landings and they had little to do. With their thin armour and small 2-pounder gun they were no use in a tank battle and for reconnaissance most men preferred a jeep. You could at least jump out of it.

General Eric Bols landed in a Horsa glider on LZ 'P' within 100 yards of Kopenhof Farm, which he had chosen off the map as his headquarters. As he and his ADC jumped down from the glider door, men of the American 513rd Parachute Infantry were just finishing off the German garrison of the farm. Two gliders were burning in the next field and the ammunition inside was making a noise like a fierce battle. Staff officers, clerks and signallers began to stream in from the 21 gliders of divisional headquarters and by 11.15am the radio sets were through to brigades. 3rd and 5th Parachute Brigades reported good progress and General Bols heard from Brigadier Bellamy in person that his glider brigade were on all their objectives. Colonel Chubby Faithful, the Commander Royal Artillery, reported that contact was made with the guns of XII Corps and the RAF Forward Air Control team clocked in soon afterwards.

It was a moment of exhilaration and relief for Eric Bols. His plan was working, his brigades were on the ground in the right place and they had already captured most of their objectives. His rear headquarters, established by Colonel Oliver Poole in a near-by farm, joined him at Kopenhof during the afternoon and at the same time General Bols heard that the leading battalions of 15th Scottish Division had reached the 3rd and 5th Parachute Brigades.

Although success had not been achieved without loss, it had been a picnic compared to Normandy for the parachute brigades and the whole division now eagerly awaited the order to advance eastwards.

Top left: A Royal Signals sergeant on the rear-link radio set at 6th Division headquarters. Behind him the complete radio trailer has been dug in and covered with a parachute./*IWM*

Bottom left: A staff officer at work on a map. He is wearing a remote control headset and there are two field telephones in his slit trench, comfortably lined with a parachute./*IWM*

Above: Part of 6th Division headquarters, some days later. Standing in front of the jeep is Colonel Chubby Faithfull, the Commander Royal Artillery and at the edge of the picture, General Eric Bols./*IWM*

The US 17th Airborne in Action

Colonel Edson Raff landed in a field among a lot of his own men from the 507th and, on looking round, realised that the woods were east and south-east of him, instead of north and north-west. He was also under machine gun and artillery fire from those same woods and from a village 500 yards to the east. This had to be Diersfordt and they were therefore some way north-west of their proper Drop Zone 'W'. Away to the north he could see a battery of 150mm guns firing and after sending off a party to destroy them, he set about clearing the woods and the village. By 11.00 the village was theirs with 340 prisoners, including a Colonel, and they had killed another 55 of the enemy in the fighting.

In the village Raff met Major Paul Smith with another large group of the 1st Battalion, who had also been clearing the woods of German gunners and machine gun positions. Raff ordered the 1st Battalion to complete the clearance of Diersfordt and to capture the Castle, but just as

Company A began their attack, the 3rd Battalion arrived, having dropped in the right place on DZ 'W'. Since Diersfordt Castle was their original objective, Raff gave them the job of capturing it and told the 1st Battalion to move to their planned position north of DZ 'W', as his regimental reserve.

At this moment two German tanks came out of the Castle. A Gammon bomb on the first one persuaded the crew to bale out and surrender, while a shell from the new 57mm recoilless rifle set the second tank on fire. Two companies of the 3rd Battalion opened fire on the Castle and Company C went in to clear it, room by room. Finally only one turret remained in German hands, defended by a group of officers, and after a prolonged battering by all available weapons they surrendered. They were mostly staff officers of General Straube's LXXXVI Corps and General Fiebig's 84th Infantry Division.

Below: An American parachute soldier lies dead on the drop zone./*IWM*

Left: An American parachute soldier, shot dead before he could free himself from his harness. His US flag brassard is visible, as are his reserve parachute and musette bag below it./*IWM*

Below: 507th Parachute Infantry on DZ 'W', shortly after dropping./*IWM*

Above: More of the 507th digging in
an orchard on the edge of DZ
'W'./*IWM*

By mid-afternoon the Castle and village were in American hands, together with 500 prisoners. Five tanks had been destroyed round the Castle and in the village, two by the new guns, two by medium artillery fire from west of the Rhine and one by that Gammon bomb. Bob Krell, *Yank* correspondent, who had gone with one of these tank hunting patrols, had been killed.

The 2nd Battalion 507th hit the right drop zone. From the moment of landing they were under machine gun and rifle fire from Germans in Flüren village and the woods on the north edge of the DZ. They cleared out these enemy positions and reached their final objective, the south west corner of the woods, by 11am. Private George Peters, a radio man in Company C, charged a German machine gun post single-handed, but a bullet hit him and he went down, badly wounded. Getting up again, he ran on towards the gun, only to be knocked down a second time by a burst of fire. After a moment's pause he crawled on, until he was close enough to throw grenades into the German position, killing and wounding the crew and silencing the gun. He died of his wounds a little later and was posthumously awarded the Medal of Honor.

By 2.30pm the 507th patrols had made contact with the right flank battalion of the 15th Scottish Division, the 6th Royal Scots Fusiliers, advancing from the Rhine, and a standing patrol was established down on the river bank to the south. On the same Drop Zone 'W' the 464th Parachute Field Artillery dropped at eight minutes past ten, mostly on the eastern end of the

drop zone and among the trees to the north. They too came under machine gun and rifle fire, as they landed, and at once set up three .50 calibre machine guns to cover their own 75mm howitzers, firing over open sights at the enemy in the woods 200 yards away. By noon four howitzers were in action, answering calls for fire from the infantry battalions and an hour later there were nine of them firing. The remaining three guns were damaged in the drop, but the gunners were able to make up one more serviceable piece by late afternoon.

At 2.58pm Colonel Raff reported to his division headquarters that the 507th had taken all their objectives, had captured 1,000 prisoners of war and were in contact with the British 6th Airborne Division, the 15th Scottish Division and the 1st Commando Brigade.

General Miley landed on DZ 'W' exactly as planned and found himself under small arms fire from all directions. The countryside looked exactly right, coinciding with his briefing maps, models and air photos, and in a few minutes he and his staff were in their chosen assembly area. An hour later his command post was established near the south east corner of the Diersfordt woods and he was in touch with his regiments. The news was good. They were all on or near their objectives, the enemy was disorganised and large numbers were surrendering.

In the afternoon the corps commander, General Matt Ridgway, drove up in a jeep with an escort jeep behind him, mounting a .50 calibre machine gun. Bud Miley took him north to see

General Eric Bols at Kopenhof Farm and on the way back in the twilight the convoy of three jeeps ran into a group of 20 Germans. Miley stood up in the leading jeep, shouting 'Hände hoch! Komm hier!' but, as he did so, there was the bang of a grenade behind him. He, his aide, the driver and a rifleman dived into the ditch and on looking back, saw Matt Ridgway standing behind his jeep, firing at the Germans. The machine gun in the rear jeep fired a few bursts and then they all went forward to see the score. Ridgway said 'I think I got one', but they found nobody there. The grenade had struck his jeep and a splinter had hit him below the heart, without penentrating deeply and certainly without worrying Matt Ridgway.

The 513th Parachute Infantry commander, Colonel James Coutts, was in the leading C-46 aircraft of the formation, which was struck by an anti-aircraft shell and set on fire, as they crossed the Rhine. On hitting the ground at 10.10 he looked around for the woods and farms, which he had memorised from the map and air photos, but could see none of them. All round him Horsa gliders were landing and he could see more and more British airborne soldiers, wearing their red berets. Through one of his men, who could speak German, he learned from a frightened family in a farmhouse that he was north west of Hamminkeln and about a mile and a half north of Drop Zone 'X'. His three battalions followed him,

Left: Pte George Peters.

Below: 513th on LZ 'P'. They have dug some quick slit trenches for cover from fire./*US Army*

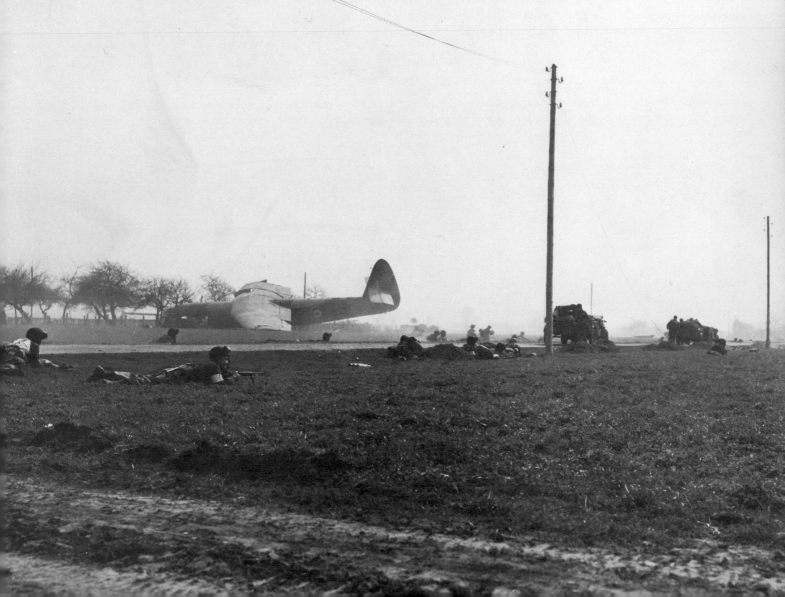

Above: A sequence of photos of the same action. A farm on LZ 'P' is held by the Germans. A British soldier is kneeling to fire, as a German runs out. In the foreground an American of the 513th lies dead, shot from the farm before he could get out of his parachute harness./*IWM*

Right: On the other side of the same farm, an American medical orderly treats a wounded man. His parachute hangs on the telephone line./*IWM*

Far right: Pte Stuart Stryker.

jumping from their C-46s over the British landing zones 'P' and 'R', and joining with the British in the destruction of the many German anti-aircraft guns and machine guns on the landing zones.

In the 1st Battalion Lieutenant Colonel Taylor, his executive officer, operations officer, adjutant and communications officers were all missing at first and the battalion were rallied under heavy fire by Lieutenant Cosner. Moving his group to the south-west, he collected many more men of the battalion and organised a position of all round defence. There, at 12.30pm, he was joined by the regimental commander, Colonel Coutts, Lieutenant Colonel Miller of the 2nd Battalion, and a lot of other men. Coutts now put his own intelligence officer, Captain Ivy, in command of the 1st Battalion and sent him off to their planned position just south of Drop Zone 'X', as his regimental reserve.

Lieutenant Colonel Miller's 2nd Battalion were able to form up as a battalion in half an hour and set about clearing the drop zone of the many Germans in every farm and wood. Moving south

east and dodging Horsa gliders as they went, they came to the railway beyond Kopenhof Farm. Here Company E attacked the German garrison of another large farm house, but their leading platoon were caught by machine gun fire and went to ground, taking heavy casualties all the time. Private Stuart Stryker, armed with an M1 carbine, ran forward to the head of this platoon and, urging the men to their feet, led them forward at a run against the farm. Twenty-five yards further on Stryker was seen to fall, riddled with bullets, but the platoon went on to capture the farm, take 100 prisoners and release three American aircrew. Stryker was killed instantly and was later awarded the Medal of Honor. Eventually the 2nd Battalion worked their way through the woods to their final objective, the west edge of the Diersfordter Wood, between the 507th and the British 3rd Parachute Brigade, where they made contact with the British 9th Parachute Battalion.

Lieutenant Colonel Kent's 3rd Battalion, 513th, assembled in three main groups and thinking that they were on the correct drop zone, set off to the north east to find the River Issel and their final positions along its bank. After ten minutes they were so close to Hamminkeln that they realised where they were and changed course to the south-east. By 4pm they were holding the river line, with the Royal Ulster Rifles on their left and the 194th Glider Infantry on the right.

As the 513th came down on to Landing Zones 'P' and 'R' two parachutes were seen to tangle and fall like a stone. The two men had had doubly bad luck, for when they were picked up, they were found to have been shot in the air as well as killed by the impact. A luckier man with a taller story was Sergeant Curtis Gadd, for whom the Divisional History claims that, from his parachute on his way down, he shot at a German soldier on a galloping horse — and hit him.

Throughout the morning Colonel Coutts and his battalions wondered what had happened to their gunners. In fact the 466th Parachute Artillery had dropped accurately on Drop Zone 'X' at 10.25am, to find themselves under close range fire from 76 and 20mm guns and 13mm and 7.62 machine guns. They were entirely on their own, instead of being in the middle of their own parachute infantry battalions. All the officers in one battery were killed or wounded in the first few minutes, but in half an hour the gunners had cleared the area, captured a battery of ten field guns, and got several of their own guns in action, firing over open sights at point blank range. By noon the whole battalion was in action with all their 12 howitzers ready to answer calls for fire. They had killed 50 of the enemy and captured 320 prisoners, ten field guns, eight 20mm and 18 machine guns.

As the WACO gliders of the 194th Glider Infantry came in to land on Landing Zone 'S' at 10.30am, they met heavy fire from several batteries of 20mm flak guns; from field and

Left: Beside the farm a German half-track, probably from the Battle Group Karst, burns after being hit by a bazooka./*IWM*

Below: The garrison of the farm are searched, before being marched away. They are mostly men from the Luftwaffe./*IWM*

Top right: The women of the farm leave their burning home with what they can carry./*IWM*

Bottom right: A dead American in a ploughed field. In the background are two Horsa gliders./*IWM*

medium artillery and 88mm dual purpose guns; and from mortars and machine guns all over their landing zone. It was a scene of wild confusion, as 570 gliders came in to land from every direction. Practically all of them were hit by flak or by machine gun fire and 26 of them were so shot up on the ground that their crews could not unload them. Another 100 crash-landed, breaking off under-carriages, wings and tails as they careered through fences, hit trees, telephone poles and houses, or collided with other gliders. As the men piled out there was little question of an orderly assembly, until the enemy gunners had been eliminated, and a series of small battles broke out all over the area, as each glider squad attacked the nearest Germans. The continued landing and crashing of gliders, the loud, cracking explosion of 88mm shells, the hammering of the German multi-barrelled 20mm guns and the rattle of machine gun and rifle fire mingled with dust and smoke to make a noisy and confusing battle picture.

The 2nd Battalion 194th Glider Infantry had the task of holding the line of the Issel canal from the river to Wesel. Their glider pilots gave them a good, concentrated landing in the south east corner of Landing Zone 'S' close to their objective and Company G, the first on the ground, were at once in action against enemy batteries. One of their number, Private Andrew Adams, knocked out a Mark IV tank with a bazooka. The next to land, Company E, had a platoon ready to move in 15 minutes and together with Company F, led by Captain Robert Dukes,

133

they attacked a German command post. The garrison hardly had time to realise what was happening and as their commanding officer, a full colonel, was being led away a prisoner, his clerk dashed out of the dug-out shouting 'Sir, Sir, you forgot your maps.'

As Lieutenant Colonel Timmes got his 2nd Battalion mortars and machine guns into action on the landing zone to cover his move forward to the line of the canal, Private Robert Flynn was moving ahead of the battalion on a liberated bicycle. Spotting two Mark IV tanks, he pedalled back as fast has he could to warn the leading companies. Private Geist in Company G let one of the tanks come on to within fifteen yards from his ditch, before destroying it with a bazooka round, and Private William Palowida got the second one in the same way. By 12.30pm Timmes's companies were digging in on the line of the Issel canal and during the rest of the day had little difficulty in beating off three counter-attacks by the Karst Anti-Airlanding Group. In one of these fights Robert Weber scored a long range hit on a third tank with a high angle shot from his bazooka, setting the tank on fire. The

Far left, top: A burned out Waco and Jeep./*IWM*

Far left, bottom: A Waco on its nose. In the foreground is a supply drop container./*IWM*

Left: The British 6-pounder anti-tank gun, used by the Americans, is driven off the LZ./*IWM*

Below: American glider men try to salvage equipment from a wrecked glider./*IWM*

Above: The 194th leaving their gliders on LZ 'S'./*IWM*

Right: An American soldier, killed by the enemy's fire on LZ 'S'. /*IWM*

forward observer from the 681st Glider Field Artillery, Lieutenant Herman Lemberger, helped five wounded men of Company G by giving them first aid, and during the last of the enemy attacks, brought down the effective fire of his regiment on to the enemy tanks, losing his life from the enemy's fire in doing so.

The 1st Battalion assembled quickly after a good, accurate landing and moved out to the River Issel. Company A were digging foxholes round the bridges over the river within 30 minutes of landing and preparing the bridges for demolition in case of a serious counter-attack. On the left Company C were troubled at first by Germans in a farm near the river, until a glider load of men from Company B stormed the farm with grenades and rifles and captured two 88mm guns.

Major Taylor's 3rd Battalion landed near the eastern end of Landing Zone 'S' and they had a tough time, clearing the area of groups of German gunners and machine gun posts, as they fought their way to the western end of the landing zone and their final positions in the south east corner of the Diersfordter woods. They were all there by 4.30pm and spent most of the evening and night clearing the woods of Germans, destroying one Mark IV tank in the process and damaging another.

By noon Colonel James Pierce was in full control of all his battalions. They were holding firmly the eastern and southern flanks of the 17th Division's area. During the day his 194th Glider Infantry had lost 159 men killed and more than 500 wounded, but they had destroyed or captured 42 German guns, ranging in calibre from 155mm to 75mm, two flak-wagons, five self-propelled guns and ten tanks, as well as taking 1,150 prisoners.

Both the 681st and 680th Glider Field Artillery had a series of sharp fights on their landing zones and used their guns at point blank range, firing over open sights from beside their gliders. Once in action, supporting the glider infantry battalions, they were several times attacked by enemy groups, and the glider pilots attached to them played a useful part in beating off these attacks.

By midday all the 17th Division artillery observers were in contact with British guns west of the Rhine and it was these field and medium regiments of the 53rd Welsh Division, which provided most of the support for the Americans that day. By noon too, air observation light aircraft, American L 19s and British Austers, were flying over both airborne divisions and the artillery network of radio and telephone links was well on the way to completion.

The 139th Airborne Engineers and the divisional troops on Landing Zone 'N' met the same sort of resistance and took a number of prisoners and guns. In Company A the commander suffered a broken arm from an anti-

Below: Waco gliders on LZ 'N'. In the left foreground is a British Horsa with one wing off and just right of centre is the massive wing-span of a Hamilcar.

aircraft shell while still in the air and his second in command took over. Company B landed in a close pattern and lost no time in clearing houses and farms on the landing zone of their German defenders, killing twenty of them and capturing a battery of 105mm guns, three half-tracks, a number of cars and trucks and 95 prisoners. In Company C, a glider, loaded with explosives, was hit in mid-air and exploded, but the rest of them cleared their part of the landing zone without much difficulty. Three more gliders were shot to pieces on landing, three crashed with the loss of the loads on board and 15 more crash-landed, but without damage to the vehicles and equipment inside them. A serious loss was their medical glider. Landing close by a farmhouse full of 40 Germans, it was hit by a mortar bomb and by rifle and machine gun fire. The jeep driver was killed and the jeep and medical stores were burned, but the doctor and his sergeant survived to set up the battalion aid post.

Major Kenny's 224th Medical Company, landing at 12.25pm in 50 gliders, none of which carried Red Cross markings, lost two officers shot dead in the first five minutes and 14 more men killed and 30 wounded or injured before the day was over. They set up their casualty clearing station on the western end of Landing Zone 'N' and were in business an hour after landing. The field surgical team were kept hard at it all day and by nightfall they had treated 33 men for injuries received on landing, 175 for slight wounds and 117 more serious cases. These included two maxillo-facial, six abdominal and seven sucking wounds and eight compound fractures. They had planned to use glider-snatch for the evacuation of the wounded and had the necessary gear with them. On this occasion however there was no need to use it, as the Rhine ferries were operating by the evening and the next day the serious cases were driven back over the river. German prisoners were used as stretcher bearers and to dig shelter trenches and a number of German doctors and medical orderlies were put to work on their own wounded.

Close behind the last troop carrier formation came the 240 B-24 Liberator bombers of the United States Eighth Air Force, each loaded with 2½ tons of supplies, packed into 20 containers, double the load of a C-47. They had taken off

Below: Two men of an American glider unit. The nearest has a shell dressing on the back of his helmet and is carrying a sub-machine gun. He also seems to be wearing a British helmet. His mate is taking cover, probably for the photographer's benefit, as he is still smoking. He has an M1 carbine./*US Army*

Left: Two medical orderlies, one wearing a Red Cross cloth, wheel in a casualty from the Landing zone./*IWM*

Below: Another casualty is helped along./*IWM*

Right: A parachute soldier with a wounded foot at the door of a dressing station./*IWM*

Below: An American dressing station./*IWM*

from their bases in Norfolk and Suffolk at 9.10am, the big four-engined aircraft rolling down the runways at one minute intervals. Following the same route as the troop carriers but flying much faster at 160mph and at 3,000 feet, half of them were to drop their supplies to the 17th Division on Drop Zone 'W' and the remaining 120 to the 6th Division just to the west of Hamminkeln. They were flying 'nine ship elements' vics of threes, like the troop carriers, and except for five planes, which dropped their loads on the wrong side of the Rhine, the all made accurate runs to their dropping zones. Over the river they were down to 300 feet and this massed formation of heavy bombers, sweeping low over the airborne divisions, drowning the sounds of battle with the thunder of nearly a thousand engines, made a lasting impression on the men watching from the woods and fields. Their supplies were scattered all over the Diersfordter woods, partly because of the speed and low altitude and partly because the containers in the fuselage had to be pushed out by hand. An awkward container, or a fouled line, indeed any delay in the six seconds allowed, meant a wide dispersion on the ground. There was some risk, too, in pushing these containers out and one man was whipped out of the open hole with the container he was despatching. The 17th Division

reported that they picked up half their drop of 306 tons and the 6th collected 80% of their 292 tons. A lot more was found and used by units without report and the drop was certainly successful.

Up to the drop zones they had met no enemy fire, but as soon as they were clear of the ground held by the two airborne divisions, they ran into flak, mostly 20mm, and machine gun fire, worse than anything they had experienced on their many bombing missions. In spite of their armour, 15 of the B-24s were shot down and 104 of them were damaged, before they re-crossed the Rhine on their return flight — a loss ratio seven times greater than that of the troop carriers, which had flown to LZ 'N' a few minutes earlier. Some planes were hit just beyond the drop zones and other flew beyond the Issel, before making their turn for home, so exposing themselves at low level to German gunners who had avoided the preliminary anti-flak bombardment or capture by the airborne divisions.

At 5pm on 24 March DUKWS, amphibious trucks, began crossing the Rhine loaded with supplies of ammunition, petrol, food and medical stores for the two airborne divisions and the flow of wounded men westwards over the river was in full swing by early morning. On March 25 the 6th Airborne Division set off on its long march across

Above: A C-47 snatches a glider — trailing a hook on a cable, attached to a drum and clutch in the aircraft. The glider tow-rope is raised on two poles and engaged by the hook. The glider accelerates from standstill to 110mph in 5 seconds./*IWM*

141

Above: Two B-24 Liberator bombers, flying low over the landing zones to drop their supply containers./*IWM*

Left: A photograph, taken from one of the B-24's, of a Horsa glider completely smashed on LZ 'P'./*IWM*

Above right: The bridges over the Rhine are open and the 6th Division's vehicles move up to join their units. In the background are containers from the B-24 supply drop./*IWM*

Right: An American M10 tank-destroyer moves forward past a group of prisoners and two Horsas — a 75mm gun and a .50 calibre Browning machine-gun on the turret./*IWM*

Germany as part of the British VIII Corps, which only ended when they reached the Baltic coast early in May. They returned to England that same month and in September 1945 moved to Palestine, where they served on until disbandment in 1947.

The 17th Airborne Division with the 513rd Parachute Infantry riding on the Scots Guards' Churchill tanks, moved rapidly eastwards to capture Munster and then swung south and west to play their part in clearing the Ruhr of the last German resistance. By June they were back in France, billeted round Nancy, and being rapidly broken up as men went home on demobilisation or were transferred to other divisions. The remnants of the 17th embarked at Marseilles in September 1945 and the division was finally disbanded in Boston that same month.

In the official history *The United States Army in World War II* it is suggested that there was no need for Operation Varsity, that the capture of the high ground east of the Rhine could have done at less cost by ground troops and that there was no gain from the airborne landings in the speed of construction of the Rhine bridges. In the British 6th Airborne Division the cost in blood on 24 March amounted to 347 dead and 731 wounded with a further 313 missing, most of whom turned up later on. The two RAF Groups, Nos 38 and 46, lost 23 aircrew and in the Glider Pilot Regiment 173 men were killed or missing and 77 were wounded.

The United States 17th Airborne Division casualty figures for the two days, 24 and 25 March, were 393 dead and 834 wounded, 80

men were missing and there is no record of how many of them turned up. In the US Army Air Forces the groups of IX Troop Carrier Command lost 169 aircrew killed or missing and another 116 wounded. 35 of their glider pilots were killed and 37 wounded or injured. The difference in the impact of casualties on the two Air Forces is highlighted still more by the aircraft loss figures — only seven British tug aircraft destroyed and 32 damaged out of 440 taking part, whereas the US Army Air Forces lost 46 C-47 and C-46 troop carriers and 15 B-24 bombers out of a total of 1,395 aircraft engaged. By contrast the British glider pilots suffered much more heavily than the American and these differences are probably explained by the British glider release height of 2,500 feet and the Americans' choice of 600 feet.

The two airborne divisions together captured some 4,000 prisoners that day and probably killed and wounded another thousand. General Fiebig confirmed later that his 84th Infantry Division of 4,000 men had been eliminated almost to a man and most of the Karst Group were also destroyed. Perhaps the most important gain was the destruction of 90 German artillery pieces, ranging from 155mm down to 76mm, a large number of 20mm guns in multiple

mountings and hundreds of machine guns. It seems likely that the undisturbed fire power of these guns might well have held up the advance from the Rhine of the assault divisions of XII Corps and delayed the construction of the bridges. As it was, the first bridge to be completed was built by US Ninth Army engineers south of Wesel and was in use by 4.30pm. In the British XII Corps sector the first bridge, built on floating boats, capable of carrying nine tons, was ready for use at 10pm but at 2am next day, 25 March, it was damaged by enemy action and only opened again at 3pm. Nine-ton rafts were working a ferry service from as early as 6.30am on 24 March and a tank ferry was operating that evening. The fire of 90 guns, directed by observers on the high ground of the Diersfordter woods, on to the ferries and bridging sites, might have seriously delayed the whole movement of Second Army across the Rhine. Certainly General Dempsey was in no doubt about the value of the airborne landings in the establishment of his bridgehead over the Rhine. In seven days his leading troops, the 6th Airborne Division, were 40 miles on from the river and there were eight infantry, four armoured and two airborne divisions and four independent armoured brigades east of the Rhine. Six weeks later the war in Europe was over.

Below: Giles' *Daily Express* cartoon after Operation Varsity./*Daily Express*

"Am I mistaken, or did I hear one of you give a long, low whistle?"